EASTERN SPIRITUALITY
for
MODERN LIFE

We are all
here together; there
are no good religions, nor
bad religions, just different religions—
each having their own particular
vantage point of the
great way.
The true guru is within.
Your personal connection
with the source is what
all these wonderous teachings lead to.

EASTERN SPIRITUALITY for MODERN LIFE

Exploring Buddhism, Hinduism, Taoism and Tantra

DAVID POND

New Age Books

ISBN: 81-7822-199-3

First Indian Edition: Delhi, 2005

(Reprinted from *Western Seeker, Eastern Paths: Exploring Buddhism, Hinduism, Taoism and Tantra* published by Llewellyn Publications, USA)

Published by
NEW AGE BOOKS
A-44 Naraina Phase-I
New Delhi-110 028 (INDIA)
Email: nab@vsnl.in
Website: www.newagebooksindia.com

For Sale in Indian Subcontinent Only

Printed in India
at Shri Jainendra Press
A-45 Naraina Phase-I, New Delhi-110 028

Dedication

To the community of Seekers and Teachers who have kept the spiritual traditions alive in all cultures and places.

PREFACE

THREE BLIND MEN were examining an elephant and discussing its characteristics. The first man was touching the tusks and described the elephant as hard and smooth. The second blind man was exploring the elephant's belly and described it as huge, soft, and wrinkly. The third was sitting on top of the elephant and described it as broad and bony. And so it is with our search for truth. Each religion might very well see a separate aspect of truth and be blind to the others. It is clear that our shrinking world requires us to step outside of our separatist ways and seek to better understand each other. It is in this spirit that this book is written.

I see the Eastern paths as rafts in the ocean. There are times when we are in the ocean, adrift without direction, and the rafts are there. The Eastern teachings are filled with practices and techniques for accessing our inner guidance, listening to the still quiet voice within, and helping to regain our bearings. Some of them help us get to the other shore, the next stage of our consciousness growth. Some of them are helpful when we are floundering in the fog of our own bewilderment and they offer a temporary refuge. Truth resonates for each of us in a unique way—the teachings that resonate for one person are not always the same as those that would work for another. There are teachings for each temperament, each soul pattern. Trust that if you seek your true path, you will find it.

What a magical time we live in, spiritual and mystical teachings are abundant and available to all of us. We have access to books, audio and videotapes, and the Internet. This accessibility is fueling an emergence of a new Western spirituality, as our existing beliefs interact with the imported teachings from other cultures. Perhaps this blending of many of the world's religions that is occurring in the Western world today is the beginning of something good. From out of chaos, a new order arises. From what first appears as a cacophony of voices, each expressing a different belief, springs the creation of a fertile seedbed for an emerging worldview that encompasses differences.

It is not that one religion or mystical tradition is ultimately the best one; it is that there are many nuggets of truth and insights that can be gained by exploring each tradition. You needn't reject your own beliefs to explore other teachings. You also needn't take a religion or teaching in total to benefit from a particular nugget of truth that you might be able to incorporate into your practice. It is in this spirit that we will explore many of the Eastern paths, to see what we as Western seekers can benefit from.

By expanding our view to see what the teachings from other cultures offer, one can't help but be inspired by realizing that all the paths have something to offer each other. Each path looks at the big picture from a slightly different vantage point and has something unique to offer from its perspective. We are all here together; there are no good religions, nor bad religions, just *different* religions—each having their own particular vantage point of the great way.

It is with great joy that I share these explorations into Eastern mysticism. To serious practitioners of any of these paths, I mean no offense. I am not monastically trained, nor have I spent time with a guru. I've picked up these teachings in the same way of most Western seekers; wherever I can. I've taken the license to freely interpret the significance of these teachings to the Western-born. We can't escape our heritage; we can complement it with the teachings from other paths, but not escape it. Some will resonate to a specific path to the degree that it becomes their path, yet for most of us, the teachings have to be somewhat adapted to fit a Western lifestyle to be useful.

For many, the path of awakening goes along in fits and spurts. Periods of dedicated development are followed by periods of apathy and slacking off. This has to be acceptable, too. Otherwise, if you succumb to past habits and fall off your path, you may reject even the notion of being on a path itself. If we give ourselves space to fall off the path once in a while, then we get back on and eventually spend more time on than off. Momentum counts. They say that once you wake up, you can never go back to sleep. You can take little naps now and again, but never fully go back to sleep.

The legends of Eastern mysticism include many magical and wondrous realities. Psychic powers and miracle stories seem to go hand in hand with the awakening. We will explore these, but are advised not to stop there. Levitating saints, bilocation, shapeshifting, and clairvoyance . . . this is the effervescence of the path, but not the essence. Like dazzling neon lights, these magical powers capture our attention, but the question of "What is the source of this experience?" remains.

What is the source of this consciousness expressing itself as you? This focusing of the attention to the source is what all paths through the various schools of Eastern mysticism teach. Many techniques, many beliefs, yet the same question and destination—what is the source of self?

There is nothing closer than your connection to this source. Who better than you can affirm this place where you begin and the true source emerges? A teacher can point you to this place within, but ultimately you are the final authority on your connection with the Divine. The Eastern paths are various ways of awakening your own inner teacher. As you experience these different teachings, notice which ones resonate with your inner sense of truth. There are so many different paths, different styles to meet the different temperaments, karmic needs, past lives, and personal inclinations. Be willing to quest a bit, sample the menu, and then focus in on the teachings that most fit your natural way of being. And how do you know? The right teachings fit . . . you are not doing them because you should—they just work for you.

The true guru is within. Your personal connection with the source is what all these wondrous teachings lead to. So we start from the end—you are already there, and let's begin our journey to the East.

CONTENTS

LIST OF FIGURES

Acknowledgments

Although I am not monastery trained, nor have I received personal instruction from any of the following teachers, still I would like to acknowledge my spiritual lineage. Through their books, tapes, classes and workshops, the information from the following teachers has had the most profound impact on my spiritual development: Ram Dass, Yogananda, Osho, Shrunryu Suzuki, Pema Chödrön, and His Holiness the XIV Dalai Lama. Although it would be impossible to acknowledge all of the teachers and influences that have impacted the material in the development of this book, it has particularly been the influence of these core teachers that has set me on my path.

I would like to thank Jane Pond, Lucy Pond, and Richard Denner for the helpful suggestions with the Buddhism chapter. I would like to acknowledge Lynn Mitchell for reading the manuscript and her encouragement. I would like to acknowledge all of my friends at Chapter One Bookstore in Ketchum, Idaho, especially Nimagna and Ananda. Your friendship and support by hosting workshops for the past nineteen years has provided a theater for much of the material in this book to be presented publicly. I greatly value the perspective of youth that my four sons, David, Eden, Skylar, and Forest offered from reading the material.

Most of all, I would like to acknowledge my wife Laura. From having the idea for the book in the first place, to doing specific research into the teachings, to watching over the final editing, Laura has been involved with all aspects of the book. If more people were blessed with a relationship with someone like Laura, heaven on earth wouldn't seem like such a faraway ideal.

INTRODUCTION

TO APPROACH THE Eastern path is to embrace mystery. Although many of the teachings are very pragmatic in their approach of how to embrace life just as it is, what they teach about the true nature of life is much more expansive and encompassing than our typical Western view. "The Tao that can be told is not the eternal Tao," teaches the *Tao Te Ching*.[1] We are encouraged to embrace the mystery—to accept that there is much beyond our ability to understand. We learn that our rational mind is only one of the many ways of perceiving reality. We also have physical, emotional, intuitive, and spiritual capacities with which to perceive reality.

Just as our ears can only hear certain decibels within the total range of sounds, the same is true with vision; we can see light waves only within the range from red to violet, even though we know the range of light waves extends far beyond the colors we see. So it is with human consciousness. The rational mind has its built-in limits of how much it can comprehend, but that doesn't limit reality; only that which can be understood by the rational mind.

The Eastern paths have embraced these subtle realms of consciousness beyond the rational mind. By exploring their teachings, we become more familiar with the subtle states of consciousness that are just as real as the more familiar realms. Most of what we will be exploring requires more than philosophical attention; there is some doing involved, and these traditions have specific practices that one can engage in to have direct experience of the teaching. We learn the techniques for gaining a peaceful mind, for listening to the still, quiet voice within, to access the inspiration that comes from following spirit, to experience the depth of meaning by listening to the soul's needs.

Engaging these practices leads us to an experience of spaciousness. We learn to drop the walls that separate life into good and bad, right and wrong, etc. In letting go, we gain. A great peace can come from dropping the "need to know." I once heard the saying, "A mystic knows what can be known and leaves the rest as a source of wonder and awe." There is a place within each of us that is beyond judgment, and the great gift of pursuing Eastern mysticism is that it can help us to cultivate the place within ourselves that experiences great peace.

Our Western training has taught us to look for the final analysis. The Eastern paths teach us to let go of that need and, instead, to learn to rest in the observing part of the mind. We are raised to believe in a linear sense of time; everything has a start and a finish, a beginning and an end. As we approach the Eastern way of viewing life, we enter into the timelessness of cyclic time and the teachings of reincarnation and rebirth.

Growing up in a Western culture, I received an education, both in science and in religion, which fostered the belief that there was ultimately a right answer to every question in life. This leads to the belief that something, or someone, is good or bad, right or wrong, saved or not saved. These views lead to many walls between what is acceptable and what isn't. This, of course, makes perfect sense to the rational mind. If a person only listens to this level of human consciousness, this type of thinking works perfectly well. However, if you venture outside the realm of the rational mind, you will need to develop other faculties in consciousness to find your way. First and foremost is "the witness."

Cultivating the Witness

Central to all of the Eastern paths is learning to cultivate the witness point of consciousness. In and of itself, the witness is not all that mystical. If I asked you to stop reading and reflect on your general state of being at this moment, this is something we can all do. What place within you is doing the observing? This is "the witness." It is learning to reside in this witnessing place within, even while you go about your life, opening the door to other levels of consciousness.

The witness within you is not grasping, judging, nor analyzing—no, it is simply observing. By allowing yourself to observe more and reserve judgment, you open to a more spacious view of life that has room for dichotomies and differences. An expansive feeling accompanies this as you can accept so much more of life than when you held rigid views. You begin to experience the peace that accompanies seeing things as they are, instead of how you think they should be different. From the vantage point of the witness, you can observe the yin-yang nature of reality: Life is change; change is law. Knowing that life is always in a state of change frees us from attaching to rigid views of truth. That which is scientific truth today is outdated tomorrow by the latest truth, so was it really truth in the first place?

The Eastern paths have a few common denominators that are a stretch for the Western mind—meditation, reincarnation, and karma, particularly. Since these issues are a core theme of many of the paths we will explore, they deserve some exploration right up front.

Practicing Meditation

Central to all of the Eastern paths is meditation. There are many types of meditation, and they all have the core theme of quieting the thinking mind and awakening to other levels of consciousness. Meditation cannot be sidestepped with any hope of progress—it is that important. Reading and knowing about the experience isn't enough. That would be like reading about the piano, but not playing it. Where would the music come from? Without a meditation practice, where would the music of the soul come from?

Meditation for Quieting the Mind

How long you do this at first is not as important as simply doing it. If you only have a few minutes, do it anyway. Eventually you might build up to twenty minutes, but don't force that on yourself at the start.

Sit with your spine straight. If you can sit in lotus or half-lotus posture, fine, but even sitting in a chair with your feet flat on the floor will do. Bring your head into alignment with your spine, with your ears over your shoulders, as if your head were being gently pulled from above. Let your hands rest naturally on your lap, palms up to receive. You can close your eyes or leave them half open, blankly looking at a spot on the floor four feet in front of you. Relax your jaw and mouth muscles so you can breathe through your mouth and nose with ease.

Steady your breath and deepen it in a controlled, yet not forced, manner. Now simply keep your attention on your breath for the duration of the meditation. Notice the subtle rising on the in-breath and the subtle falling on the out-breath. When thoughts arise—and they will—simply notice them, but don't follow them, and return to the breath. The goal isn't to try to stop the thoughts; they will always arise—instead, you stop following the thoughts. Take special notice of the gaps between thoughts and experience the spaciousness.

Be gentle with yourself and try not to judge your experience. Just *be* with the experience. When your mind wanders, gently pull your attention back to the breath. Whatever arises, just note it, but don't analyze it. Picture your thoughts of having nothing to attach to, like champagne bubbles in a glass, rising and then gone. Enjoy the experience of *now.*

We will explore many meditation techniques throughout the book, but picture this first meditation as the basic building block of meditation.

Reincarnation and Karma

These two principles are interwoven throughout Eastern traditions, and as they are such a stretch for the Western mind, they might best be addressed right up front. Reincarnation is the belief in the eternal nature of the soul, and that it is reborn into a new personality with each incarnation. There is a part of us that never dies and is never born. It is that place within you that reincarnates in different manifestations of the same soul. It is not that the ego or personal identity is reborn; no, it is the soul that gathers the experiences from each life and learns from it. Picture life here on Earth as a classroom that the soul comes to, time and time again, through different incarnations to learn the various lessons of life on its journey toward full awakening.

Karma is intricately connected to this understanding. Karma basically means that there are consequences from each of our actions and choices, both good and not so good. All that is set into motion will eventually bear "like fruit." Each action, thought, or deed that we partake in has its consequences in our lives and those around us. Karma exists in our mind and emotions as strong imprints in the energy field, essentially creating ionization in the energy field that will eventually attract exactly the right situation to bring it back into balance. We will eventually experience in our lives every experience that our actions have caused others to experience—for good or for ill. We carry this karmic account in our energy field at all times—the sum total of all of our thoughts and actions.

When we die, this karmic account stays intact with the energy field, which doesn't die. When the next situation that perfectly matches our karmic account presents itself, we are reborn, taking up right where we left off. The effort that we put forth in previous lives manifests as natural skills and talents in this life. Where we misused our talents in previous lives manifests as challenges and difficulties in this life. Karma assures continuity. It's not as if our lives are somehow random; no, there is continuity from one life to the next based on our karmic attachments.

To apply this to our lives is to become more conscious of the consequences of our actions throughout the day. It is also thought of as a way of "accumulating merit" or good karma. Thoughts and actions that are intended to help, love, and heal others are said to improve one's karma, and thoughts, actions, and deeds that are intended to harm others create negative karma. It presents an opportunity to be more creative with life by giving us a tool for seeing the lesson at hand, and the method for cultivating the quality of life we wish to experience.

One of the subtleties of understanding and applying the understanding of karma is observing how its effect seems to be spread out through time. We can understand karma in the simple direct manifestation of "If I yell at Tom, and he yells back at me." But it is not always as direct as that. But if Tom yells at me unprovoked, and search as I might, I can't find a memory of having provoked this in Tom, then I wonder, "What is the karma of this?" However, if I expand my search and see if I can remember a time when I yelled at someone unprovoked, I'll likely come up with a memory and see the nature of how karma works. It spreads out over time and space.

When we finally realize we can't escape our own karma, then we can start taking responsibility for how our lives are unfolding. There is a lesson to be learned in everything, if we pay attention. This frees us from the "blame game," assuming that there is someone to blame for the way life is. Understanding the principles of karma, we would know there is something to be learned from every experience; in some way, the current situation is exactly perfect for what your soul needs to learn in this moment.

The ego will be throwing a tantrum over the injustice, but if you watch from the soul perspective, you know that the current situation is a perfect opportunity for you to learn from your karma. Ask yourself, "What am I meant to learn from this situation?" "Why is this appropriate for me at this time?" "How can I be a better person by facing something about myself I had not seen before?" It takes great strength of character to resist the ego's defensive attitude to the situation and to rise above one's personal reactions to the situation and observe from the vantage point of the higher self . . . it is just watching, observing; it can see what is going on. Ask from this perspective, and you'll get the clear answer—not always flattering, most often not, but the clarity of the lesson at hand is there if you're ready to see.

Of course, karma is not just our account of negative actions—it is the sum total of all our actions, good and bad. When we plant tomatoes, we get tomatoes. When we cultivate honorable actions with others, our karmic account turns positive and we start reaping the benefits of this. Basically, our life is what we make of it.

In the following chapters we will explore Buddhism, Hinduism, Taoism, and Tantra teachings. It immediately becomes apparent that although there is some common ground, Eastern mysticism encompasses a wide variety of teachings and beliefs. Some of the teachings are very simple, almost austere; others are very mentally elaborate. The beauty of this is that there is a teaching and path suited for each person's temperament. Seek and ye shall find—so let's start seeking!

Endnote

1. Stephen Mitchell (trans.), *Tao Te Ching,* p. 1.

BUDDHISM

THE ORIGINS OF Buddhism can be traced to the historical Buddha in the sixth century B.C.E. This singular man set forth teachings that have spawned a religion now practiced all over the globe. What is interesting about the Buddha's story is that he had mortal parents, like you and me. He came from a royal family, but nonetheless, a mortal one. He was married, he had a child, and he became enlightened. He taught that we all have this same Buddha nature and presented teachings on how to live like a Buddha. That he was born a mortal birth and experienced the same passions and emotions as us make his teachings seem accessible—you can't be born a virgin birth, but you can learn to be like Buddha.

Enlightenment in this life is openly talked about and the expressed intent of many a Buddhist. This openness to enlightenment and the way it is discussed and written about in Buddhist circles makes it somehow more tangible. Lama Surya Das, in *Awakening the Buddha Within,* writes:

> Enlightenment means an end to directionless wandering through dreamlike passages of life and death. It means you have found your own home Buddha. How does the Buddha feel? Completely comfortable, at peace and at ease in every situation and every circumstance with a sense of true inner freedom, independent of both outer circumstances and internal emotions.[1]

Buddhism is unique among religions in that it posits no particular definition of God. It's not that Buddhists reject God, but they resist *defining* God, believing definition limits, and God is beyond all limits, thus can't be conceptualized. The end result is that Buddhism is not in conflict with other religions. One could be a Christian or a Hindu and practice Buddhism without conflict. There's nothing to conflict *with*.

This gives Buddhism a broad base of appeal. One doesn't have to renounce their current beliefs to practice Buddhism. It's not like that. The Buddhist teachings are more about how to live in harmony in this life.

Buddhism begins with the story of Buddha's life, born in 564 B.C.E. to a royal family as a prince. His name can be puzzling as he is alternately called Buddha, Siddhartha, Gautama, and Shakyamuni in the literature. To understand these various monikers, it can be seen that he was born in the country of Shakyas, in northern India, to the royal clan of Gautama, and was given the name of Siddhartha, Prince Siddhartha. He became the Buddha ("Awakened One") with his enlightenment. His life story is well documented in many fine books, which can be found in the suggested reading list at the end of this chapter. I will simply summarize the story to set the stage.

Buddha: *The Awakened One. When we speak of Buddha, we most often refer to Shakyamuni Buddha, Prince Siddhartha awakened. But Buddha is also a state of consciousness available for all. There are many Buddhas, and we are told we all have Buddha Nature, the same Buddha Nature.*

It is said that when the Buddha's mother, Maya, was pregnant, she had a dream of rising out of her body and encountering a white elephant that entered her body on the right side. She told her dream to her husband, the king, and he asked his wise men about its meaning. He was told that his son would be a great soul, a powerful leader, but what direction he would take was not certain. If he stayed with the king, he would also become a great ruler and expand the kingdom, and it would flourish. However, if he became interested in the contemplative life, he would abandon his heritage and the throne, and become a Buddha, an enlightened being and spiritual teacher.

When the king learned of this, he became concerned about losing his son to the contemplative life, so he devised a plan to keep him from ever wanting anything, or becoming contemplative. No wealth was spared in providing Prince Siddhartha all of the luxuries and comforts of life while being protected from any hardships whatsoever. The king went so far as to hide anything that hinted of problems and suffering from the prince. He was never allowed to see sick, old, or dying people. He lived in a veritable pleasure palace, and was constantly attended to by beautiful women to keep him from wanting anything.

When Prince Siddhartha was in his twenties, and had shown no signs of leaving the kingdom, the king thought it was time he learned to rule. He arranged a marriage with a beautiful girl, and the two had a son together. The king hoped that Siddhartha's becoming a father would motivate him to start becoming more of a leader.

At the same time, Siddhartha became restless to know more of what was going on outside the palace walls. On one of his outings, he happened to see an old man, bent with age and struggling to walk up the street. He had never seen an old person and asked his attendant, "What is this?" His attendant told him, "Why, master, everyone gets old; this is what will happen to all of us."

This set Siddhartha to contemplating. On successive trips, he saw a sick person and a funeral procession with a corpse. When he asked his attendant about this, he was told again, "Why, master, old age, sickness, and death will happen to everyone." This sent Siddhartha into even deeper contemplation. He had never known of such things as suffering, sickness, and death, and to think this was going to happen to everyone gave him great cause to contemplate.

On yet another outing, Siddhartha noticed a different looking fellow wearing little clothes. Upon inquiring, he discovered he was a wandering mendicant, a *sadhu,* one who has renounced worldly life to contemplate life's meaning. That there were people like this, contemplating the meaning of life, shook him to his core, and the seed was planted. At twenty-nine, after much struggling within as to whether to leave his kingdom, wife, and child, Siddhartha left it all and joined the mendicants in the forest.

Hinduism was well established in India at this time, and there was already a rich spiritual tradition of introspection, including an understanding of reincarnation, the eternal nature of the soul, and an understanding of karma. The path of the mendicants was in practicing complete renunciation of bodily existence so one could center the attention on God, purge oneself of all negative karma, and be free from *Samsara.*

Samsara: *Eternal rebirth into the realms of suffering, old age, and sickness. Caused by the attachments and desires for worldly experiences, the wheels of Karma keep one locked in the realm of illusion.*

The mendicants practiced asceticism to free their attention to God. Mortification of the body by starving it, giving it no attention, renouncing all pleasures of the senses, eating the most meager sustenance to just barely keep the body alive—this was considered the truest of paths. Stay in the elements, protect the body from nothing, let it bake and burn, dry and crack, and anchor the attention on God.

This the former prince did in earnest. Wearing only a loincloth, he followed the path of complete bodily neglect for six years. His dedication was admired by the other renunciants and he became respected as one who would surely attain *Nirvana.* His constant quest was in searching for the cause and liberation of suffering.

Nirvana: *The state of freedom from Samsara. Liberated from the illusion of separateness, one experiences the Divine bliss of transcending duality. The experience of oneness with all creation.*

After six years, Gautama had absolutely quieted the fires of his desires, he was free from attachments, longings, and ambitions, yet he still didn't feel absolutely free. He knew he must find his own way. When a girl from the local village offered him food, he accepted and his friends believed he had fallen from the way. But Gautama was resolved and renounced even the path of the renunciant to find his own way. He went to the famous Bodhi tree, and sat under it with the intent to stay there until he became enlightened.

Legend has it that as he approached the final stages of enlightenment, the forces of Mara (similar to the devil; the tempter; doubt) launched an all out assault against him to try to defeat his efforts. From temptations, to threats, to all out attacks, Mara appeared in various guises to throw off the soon-to-be Buddha from seeing beyond all illusions. In each instance, the awakening

Buddha saw through Mara's tactics, named him for what he was, and by renouncing him, defeated him.

Gautama then became the Buddha. He saw beyond the illusion of all separateness. Having completely liberated himself from his consciousness anchored in his body, he was free to explore thousands of his past lives, in favorable and unfavorable births, in animal and human births. He experienced complete enlightenment and total realization of all.

He sat completely absorbed in this transcendent state for days and traced the origins and causes of each of these lives and lessons learned. His insights were born from the awareness that all that comes into form eventually dies. That which rises, falls. He saw that investing your life in anything temporary inevitably leads to loss, as it dissolves back into the oneness. In his days of absorption in this elevated state, great compassion was born in him for all sentient beings. He wished to liberate all from suffering, and thus he formulated the first *Dharma* teachings to help others come into this revelation.

Dharma: *Truth. The essence of things as they are. The Buddha's teachings of the way toward realization.*

He first went and rejoined his friends in the forest to teach them the way. Their skepticism was overcome by the sheer presence of his being, and they became his first disciples. The first *Sangha* was formed. The Buddha was now thirty-five years old and would spend the remaining forty-five years of his life walking the dusty roads of India teaching the Dharma and gathering a spiritual community said to number in the tens of thousands.

Sangha: *Spiritual community; those who support your spiritual growth. In the formal sense, Sangha is monastic, the community that has taken the same vows. Applied to everyday life, these are the people who remind you of your spiritual path.*

To join Buddha's Sangha, all one had to do was take the vows:

> I take refuge in the Buddha.
> I take refuge in the Dharma.
> I take refuge in the Sangha.

These are called the three jewels, or gems, of Buddhism. Called the refuge prayer, it is most useful in any type of distress. You take refuge in your original innocence. It is not the historical Buddha you take refuge in, it is Buddha Nature, *your* Buddha Nature, the same as Buddha's Buddha Nature. You take refuge in the place in you that has never been soiled, hurt, or defiled in any way by your life experiences.

Taking refuge in the Dharma is aligning with the teachings. The teachings are like a raft in the ocean. When we are floundering around in the ocean being tossed and turned by every wave, the Dharma is like a raft, a refuge. You align with the teachings and they work. That is what they are there for. Sometimes we want to jump into the ocean to experience the depths and powers of passions, but when we are floundering, the Dharma is there. When you take refuge in the Dharma, you realize what a blessing it is that the teachings have been handed down through the ages and are available to us; not just Buddhist teachings, all authentic teachings. Thank God, or Goddess, or Buddha, that they are there. Take refuge in them.

When you take refuge in the Sangha, you align with a web of support for your practices, both visible and invisible. This taking refuge in right relationships with others who are also attempting to live more consciously leads to aligning with kindred spirits who support your path. Meditating and doing spiritual practices with others can intensify and deepen the experience. A group mind emerges that both intensifies and supports individual experiences. This aspect of the Sangha makes sense, but there is the invisible Sangha that one also takes refuge in. We do not evolve alone. We are all individually evolving within the sphere of human consciousness and our individual growth adds to the collective as we are also influenced by other people's growth.

The invisible community also extends into the past. All those who have practiced this same path through the ages support our individual practice. All the meditators and practitioners since Buddha, all involved with this same path and techniques, have created a groove in the collective consciousness. When you take refuge in the Sangha, you can draw on both this community of outer support and the invisible support of all those who have practiced before you, creating a strong foundation you can take refuge in.

A spin-off of this is the belief that you can call on the Buddhas at anytime, and they will be there for you immediately. When you are following your path and your intent is clear, the support is there in times of need.

The Branches of Buddhism

Buddhism has grown throughout the world and merged with the teachings of the existing traditions, blossoming into new forms. It has become the dominant religion all throughout Southeast Asia, China, Japan, and into Tibet, but now is also practiced throughout the world. The lack of rigid dogma allows Buddhism to be somewhat amorphous, and it mutates and takes on a new form within the different cultures where it has emerged.

Different traditions have developed as Buddhism flowered in these various regions. The two main divisions of Buddhism are Theravada and Mahayana. Within the Mahayana tradition, various branches have emerged with Vajrayana, or Tibetan Buddhism, and Zen being dominant.

Theravada, sometimes referred to as Southern Buddhism because of where it has flourished (Korea, Vietnam, Thailand, etc.), maintains a strict allegiance to the original teachings of Buddha. Theravada means "the way of the elders." Allegiance to the vows, the precepts, and the practices of meditation is the way.

Theravada is also known as *Hinayana,* meaning "lesser raft"—this name is not used as much due to the connotations. I once heard a monk from the Mahayana tradition describe the difference between the two that implied a great deal of judgment, "Hinayana, meaning 'lesser raft,' is only concerned with personal enlightenment. *Mahayana,* on the other hand, meaning 'the great raft,' is concerned with everyone's enlightenment." There was certainly an air of superiority in his statement.

This is both unfair and untrue. That which is explicit in Mahayana is implicit in Theravada. All of Buddhism is based on compassion for all living beings. The intention is the same; how it is achieved is different.

Mahayana, sometimes known as Northern Buddhism (China, Tibet, Japan), incorporates the teachings of evolving Buddhism. The focus of Mahayana is to liberate suffering for all beings. Vajrayana (also known as Tibetan Buddhism) is part of the Mahayana tradition, but developed its own unique expression in Tibet. Zen developed strongly in Japan and focuses on the specific meditation techniques to quiet the mind, so one can become attuned to the Buddha Nature. Unique to Zen is the tradition of *koans* as a meditational focus to liberate the mind.

The essence of Zen is in training to use meditation techniques to quiet the mind and ultimately become of aware of one's Buddha nature. The meditation practice in Zen is called *zazen*, or simply "sitting," and is considered to be the core practice. It is training in living beyond the dualistic mind of good or bad, right or wrong, etc. Through the practice of zazen, one can directly experience this unitive state of consciousness; everything is within itself and therefore nothing is judged, only observed. This practice leads to the development of what is called "empty mind"—able to receive everything and hold on to nothing.

The Five Precepts: *The precepts can be likened to the Ten Commandments, and are the vows for living mindfully in the world:*

1. *The vow of* not harming or killing. *Born out of awareness that suffering is caused by the destruction of life, and the Buddhist practitioner vows not to condone any acts that create harm in the world.*
2. *The vow of* not taking that which doesn't belong to you. *This is extended to not condoning the exploitation of others, or the environment. A further extension of this precept is to practice generosity toward those in need.*
3. *The vow of* not misusing the senses. *This particularly relates to sexuality, and the practitioner vows to be responsible with his or her sex life, and to help protect others from sexual abuse.*
4. *The vow of* refraining from wrong speech. *This includes not saying anything that you do not know to be true, or thinking thoughts or using words that could hurt another. An extension of this is cultivating listening skills and refraining from mindless chatter.*
5. *The vow of* refraining from ingesting any substances that might cloud the mind. *This includes substances that give a false sense of euphoria or inhibit seeing things as they are.*

Zen teaches that our original nature is pure. If we can lessen the grip of our everyday mind with its concern and worries, fears and hopes, memories and plans, then we can become aware of our true nature, the "Big Sky Mind."

Koan: *A puzzle for the mind to solve, which tricks the mind into enlightenment. "What is the sound of one hand clapping?" and "What did your face look like before your ancestors were born?" are examples of koans to get the mind to consider what it normally can't.*

The Four Noble Truths

All of these schools have their common origin in Buddha's original teachings called "the Four Noble Truths and the Eightfold Path."

1. In life, there is suffering

This word "suffering" needs some discussion. This translation creates an image that is not acceptable for many. The original word used by Buddha was *Dukka.* Huston Smith, in his book *World's Religions,* writes, "The word was used in Buddha's day to refer to wheels whose axles were off-center, and bones that had slipped from their socket. . . . The exact meaning of the First Noble Truth, therefore, comes down to this: Life as typically lived is out of joint. Something is awry. Its pivot is not true, this restricts movement, (blocks creativity), and causes undue friction (interpersonal conflict)."[2]

This is helpful for many of us who hear that Buddhism is based on suffering and immediately shy away from it because of the heavy connotations. That in life there is Dukka, we can understand.

2. Suffering is caused by desires and attachments

The teachings of Buddha are based on the principle of impermanence: All that is born, dies; all that arises into form eventually dissolves. It follows that when we desire something, or are attached to that which is impermanent, the eventual loss leads to suffering, disappointment, Dukka.

3. The way to end suffering is to end desires and attachments

This at first seems too obvious, like the statement, "The way to quit smoking is to stop smoking." True, but not always easy. That it is stated as one of the Four Noble Truths unequivocally points the way and encourages us to know that it can be done. This does not mean that we shouldn't enjoy the beauty and delight of the material world. But it does mean that we should not anchor our attention on that which is impermanent. We are encouraged to enjoy the beauty of a moment, but not hold on to it.

4. The way to end desires and attachments is by following the Eightfold Path

The Eightfold Path outlines a method for living life that liberates one's attention from desires. It is training in a lifestyle that is free of suffering.

The Eightfold Path

These eight paths provide a formula for conscious living. They fall into three categories of wisdom training, ethics training, and meditation training. Right View and Right Intention belonging to wisdom training; Right Speech, Action, and Livelihood belonging to Ethics training, and Right Effort, Mindfulness, and Concentration being part of the Meditation training.

1. Right View 2. Right Intention	(Wisdom Training)
3. Right Speech 4. Right Action 5. Right Livelihood	(Ethics Training)
6. Right Effort 7. Right Mindfulness 8. Right Concentration	(Meditation Training)

Let's look at them in more detail.

Right View

This could be called "Knowing the truth of the way things are." Basically, accepting the Four Noble Truths and the principle of impermanence.

Right Intention

The first level of this is obvious; setting your intentions clearly on consciously living the Eightfold Path. This harkens to the saying "Many are called, but few are chosen." The path to freedom is available for everyone, but if you don't set your intent in that direction, aimless inattention takes over.

The second level of Right Intention is born out of the compassion that Buddhism is based on. "Good in the Beginning, Good in the Middle, and Good at the End." This is a method for setting your intentions. "Good in the Beginning" is a reminder to offer any good that comes from your activity to have a ripple effect and do some good in the world for others. "Good in the Middle" is to remind yourself in the middle of activity not be grasping for that which is not in the moment. "Good at the End" is another opportunity to offer any benefit that has come from your experience to spread out into the world. "Good in the Beginning, Good in the Middle, and Good at the End" is a way to keep your ego subdued and in right alignment with Right Intention. It's a method of sharing the merit. As an example, before you meditate, you could pledge that any good that may come from your meditation spread out into the world. During your meditation, you could remember to drop any aspirations, and simply *be* with your meditation. At closure, you could once again dedicate any benefit that came from your experience to spread out and do some good in the world.

Right Speech

This is the first of the Ethics Training Paths—what you do matters. This includes what you say to others and what you say to yourself—what you allow yourself to think, being aware that the content and the energy behind your words have an impact on others, and thus your karma. Always being conscious of what you say and how you say it, realizing that with your words you have an opportunity to help, heal, love, and assist, or wound, slander, etc. In each moment, your words and thoughts can either be helpful or harmful, to others and to yourself.

In the Dhammapada (sayings from the Buddha), the first passage reads, "All that we are is the result of our thoughts. With our thoughts we make the world. If a man speaks or acts with a harmful thought, trouble follows him as the wheel follows the ox that draws the cart . . . If a man speaks or acts with a harmonious thought, happiness follows him as his own shadow, never leaving him."[3]

Right Action

This is essentially being mindful of all activities you engage in. Every activity you take part in leaves its impression on your karmic energy field, and the premise of Right Action is never taking part in that which would cause harm to self or others. This includes food and not eating that which is toxic, or causes suffering to other sentient beings. This includes indulgences and not taking part in activities that diminish one's capacity to live in alignment with the Eightfold Path. This is most often thought of as staying away from intoxicants, but it could be expanded to any activity that undermines one's resolve to live a conscious, compassionate life. Becoming conscious of what you ingest at the mental and emotional levels of life would be included. One needn't abstain from sexuality, but being mindful of not doing harm, one would not take part in sexuality that caused harm or suffering to others or one's self.

Right Livelihood

This follows from the principle of living life in a way that creates no harm. Ideally, it is finding the right type of livelihood that is honorable for you and benefits others. At minimum, it means staying away from employment that in any way creates harm for others or the environment. This could be extended to how you make money through investments, and even how you spend your money. Are you supporting companies that somehow create harm in the world? Becoming conscious of your earning and spending of money as a spiritual practice brings this dominant activity of life into your conscious practices.

Right Effort

This is the first of the Meditation Training paths. Without Right Effort, all of these teachings are just "a good idea." We could think of this as self-motivation. All of these teaching have to be set into motion by the personal will. When we think of the will, we most often associate it with activities, doing something. But this is the first of the Meditation Training exercises, so although the effort is needed to follow through on the Ethics Training, here it more specifically relates to meditation. This is to help us overcome the tendency toward spiritual laziness. I say it this way, "It seems to take a powerful amount of hell to invoke a little bit of heaven," meaning that so often we only turn to our spiritual life in times of crisis. Right Effort is needed to align with your spiritual life when crisis is not prevailing. This is when it can be sustained. If our spiritual life is only a life jacket for times of crisis, we miss the sweet nectar of engaging in spiritual practices while life is in harmony.

Even having a regular meditation practice doesn't guarantee Right Effort. We can will ourselves into a particular posture for an appointed time and still be spiritually lazy within the practice. Right Effort at the Meditation Training level requires acute attention to the meditation experience. Right Effort requires that you be absolutely awake and attentive in the meditation, not simply relaxing the mind.

Right Mindfulness

Watching and observing the mind is central to the Meditation Training. Being mindful of where the mind goes throughout your meditation session is part of this. You learn how to simply watch it, instead of identifying with it. You can't stop the mind and its thinking—that is what it does—but by becoming mindful, you can simply *observe* it rather than *follow* it. This translates into learning to become mindful throughout the day while your mind is operating. You learn to enter into the witness aspect of your mind even while taking part in mundane daily activities. This makes it possible to let go of obsessive thinking patterns that grasp us through the day.

This one can be a bit daunting. We'd like to think that what goes on in the privacy of our own mind shouldn't really matter. But Right Mindfulness teaches that it does matter, and there are karmic consequences even to what we think about. We are always creating future scripts. At first this seems limiting, or even punishing. But when understood, this teaching allows you to be creative and improve the quality of your life simply by becoming mindful of what you allow your attention to attach to and follow.

Right Concentration

Right Concentration here refers to mastering the specific meditation techniques. As in posture, breath, and the letting go of thoughts as they arise, these are specific instructions. Right Concentration refers also to allowing spaciousness in your attention. If you have too much of your attention focused on counting your breath and checking your posture, there will be no experience of spaciousness in your meditation. The advice is sometimes given to keep 25 percent of your attention on the breath and let the rest of your attention be open to the sky-like nature of your mind beyond thoughts. Or it is said to touch your breath lightly with your attention, so you may also be open to what is born out of the moment.

These eight paths, each one manageable in its own right, when practiced together, are a method for living a spiritual life—a Buddha's life.

God in Buddhism

What immediately becomes apparent in these core teachings is the absence of God. When most of us think of a religion, we associate this with some understanding of God. On this point the Buddha was strangely mute. His answer to the question of "Is there a God?" was, "Why waste your time on that which is beyond knowing? Better to focus your attention on the causes of problems in life, and how to liberate oneself from this." Buddhism is not atheistic, or denying of God, it is nontheistic, believing that any concept we hold is limited, and God is *beyond* all limitations. Buddhists therefore resist the mental constructs that we use to describe God, and instead focus on what you can do to free yourself and others from suffering.

Buddhists start with the principle of eternity. Eternity is a long time, and since this birth/death/rebirth wheel turns in eternity, we best get on with seeing what we can do to improve the quality of this life and future rebirths. Although enlightenment and freedom from rebirth is an inherent goal, it is believed that one can greatly improve the quality of future rebirths by living the Dharma—by the way we live, the deeds we do, and the thoughts we think.

The Buddhist teachings of rebirth state that the human realm is not the only realm that one can be reborn in. There is also the possibility of being reborn in the animal realms, the hungry ghost realms, and the godly realms. This helps us understand the great compassion Buddhists have for animals; after all, that dog you're petting, feeding, or neglecting may have been a mother, or a Buddha in a previous or future life! It is taught that the human realm is the most favorable of all for attaining liberation and awakening. This human realm is where we can make choices that will impact our karma and awakening. There is the encouragement to take advantage of this life as a rare and special opportunity for awakening and improving the quality of future lives.

Bodhichitta

Beyond the Four Noble Truths and the Eightfold Path, there are many teachings that support one's efforts to live in a way that constantly improves one's karma. The first of these is *Bodhichitta*—the awakened heart and mind. Bodhichitta is the soft spot within that is underneath all fears, worries, and concerns. We often try to protect ourselves from being uncomfortable, feeling far too vulnerable, so we "armor up." The core teaching of Bodhichitta is that by melting away all our resistance, and dropping our reactions to experience, we rest in the wellspring of compassion, which is our true heart. Buddhism teaches that our basic human nature is inherently good, and when we drop all effort and grasping, we rest in the cradle of loving-kindness.

Bodhichitta: *The awakened heart and mind. The natural arising of joy and compassion that comes from absolute acceptance of self and others.*

This is a bit of a stretch for many a Western-trained mind—but what a delightful stretch! The teachings of original sin, and that we've been kicked out of the Garden of Eden, have jaded us to the view of an inherently spiritual and loving nature. The Western view is one of achievement; one can achieve a higher existence by overcoming inherently human faults. The Eastern view that our true nature is loving and compassionate suggests dropping into something that is already there rather than achieving it. One teacher expressed it this way, "It is not as if one becomes enlightened as much as ceases to be deluded." The same compassionate Buddha Nature is there in you, me, and all of us; just beneath the armor—it is there. Where we might feel the wise thing to do is to protect our vulnerability, with the understanding of Bodhichitta we constantly let go of our defenses and awaken with genuine compassion for others and ourselves.

Maitri

And how is this acceptance done? With *Maitri.* Beyond forgiving, there are no judgments to forgive; this is the absolute acceptance of the highs and lows of everyone's human nature. This allows for a gentleness to emerge. When we are armored with defenses, we have difficulty accepting things as they are. We are busy pushing and shoving it around to what we think it should be. With Maitri, we begin to open to life, to accept more of what is, and spaciousness begins to be felt as the walls of judgment are removed.

We Westerners understand the "being friendly toward others" part of this equation, but unlimited friendliness toward self is quite a shift for many. This can help soften our crystalline judgments of ourselves. Many of us are much harder on ourselves than we are on others. We can let go of our judgments and accept others for who they are, yet we have standards for ourselves to which we don't quite measure up. With Maitri, we can learn to accept our own humanness as well.

We will make mistakes and periodically fall off our path. With Maitri we learn not to judge our own humanness when we wander from the high road. With loving-kindness we notice and observe, but rather than dwelling on the issue and staying attached, we come back into present time; this moment, this breath.

Maitri: *Unlimited friendliness toward self and others.*

Emptiness and Shunyata

With an understanding of *shunyata,* you gain an understanding that the true nature of your being is emptiness. You are free to accept everything, because it all dissolves within you in shunyata. Nothing sticks. It all dissolves. This allows you to accept everything; nothing is threatening, or at least, not overwhelming. You can accept the ideas of others in a non-defensive way, because there is nothing to defend. You can experience the emotions of others because they melt within you. On the next breath, you are in the next moment and all of the past dissolves in emptiness.

Shunyata: *Absolute emptiness of our true nature. Here nothing can attach, nothing can stick, and all experiences dissolve into the vast emptiness. Open clarity, free of all grasping.*

To be empty of self as the Buddha taught is learning how to not identify with the *separate* sense of self. This egolessness is an important aspect of becoming liberated from suffering. If there is no self, who will suffer? With *anatta,* there is no ego attachment to any of the experiences of life; no clinging and thus no suffering. This egolessness allows one to experience the spaciousness of one's Buddha nature.

Anatta: *To be empty of self.*

The Nature of the Mind and Meditation

And how is this done? With meditation. Without the practice of meditation, all of this is just a good idea, but it is in meditation that one directly experiences these truths. In meditation the mind begins to quiet and the true nature of our being begins to reveal itself. Resting in the wisdom nature of the mind. Not the "idea mind" of concepts, plans, and ideas, but the true nature of mind—the Buddha mind—can be tuned to.

There's a story. A monk was invited to a Buddhist society to discuss Buddhism. A woman was asking him to comment on a certain text. He asked her about her meditation practice and she said, "Goodness, I haven't time for meditation. I'm far too busy just trying to understand these Buddhist texts." To which the monk replied, "My good woman, you are like the farmer who raises chickens and goes out each morning gathering the chicken shit and leaving the eggs." A rather blunt monk, but the story gets the point across. It is only in meditation that we come to know the true nature of mind, and thus become free of its incessant ways.

Our minds race nonstop, from the moment we awaken until we fall asleep, constantly reminding us of our story. Memories, plans, desires, fantasies, grudges, hopes, on and on, from one arena to the next in a nonstop arising of more things to think about. In meditation, we give it a rest. I like to tell my mind before meditating something like this, "Look, I'll be paying attention to you for twenty-three-and-a-half hours today. For the next half hour, let me listen to a deeper voice."

In Zen, it is taught that there are two levels of mind: the everyday mind and Big Sky Mind. The everyday mind, also called "monkey mind," is our normal waking consciousness. It is the constant self-dialogue going on affirming the nature of your life. It is constantly telling your story; the memories, thoughts, plans, desires, and resentments that make up your life. Behind this everyday mind is the Big Sky Mind—serene, tranquil, and simply observing. The everyday mind, in its attempts to analyze, think, process and figure things out, is like the clouds obscuring your view of the sky. By quieting the thoughts, we dispel the clouds and the spaciousness of the open sky appears.

In zazen, one uses the mind to quiet the mind by focusing exclusively on the breath. During the out-breath, focus is on the experience of breathing out. During the in-breath one focuses on breathing in—that's it. When thoughts arise, simply let go of them and return to the breath. It is not that you can ever stop the mind from thinking, that is what it does, but with practice you can learn to not follow the thoughts; simply notice them and return to the breath. Counting is often employed as a way of holding attention to the breath. "Breathing out, one; breathing in, two," etc. Here the advice is given that if you lose yourself in thought, go back to one and start over. In Zen circles the joke is, "How do you get to two?"

By daily practice it becomes more natural to dismiss arising thoughts and spend more time in the spaciousness of Big Sky Mind, simply observing the "As-is-ness" of life. Be present; be here and now; accept the reality of everything with equal calm and equanimity. This practice translates into the everyday life, and is most beneficial when you find yourself reacting, tracking, and obsessing on certain thoughts throughout the day. The sitting practice is training for dismissing thoughts as they obscure the Big Sky Mind throughout the day. Shunryu Suzuki, in *Zen Mind, Beginner's Mind,* says, "Nothing outside of self can cause you trouble. You yourself make the waves in your mind. If you leave your mind as it is, it will become calm."[4]

In Tibetan Buddhism, it is taught that there are two levels of the mind: *Rigpa* and *Sem.* Sem is ordinary mind, the constant dialogue with the self that goes on, constantly affirming our reality by reminding us of plans, angers, problems, joys, memories, longings, and desires. "This is who I am, remember?" As if it somehow needs to be naming everything in our lives constantly for fear that it might otherwise disappear. Rigpa is the true nature of mind beyond all of these constant yammerings of the ego, or ordinary mind.

In meditation, one is learning to rest in Rigpa, Big Sky Mind. The focus of meditation is first to quiet the ordinary mind. Engaging in a practice of following and counting the breaths, letting go of thoughts as they arise, and eventually resting in Rigpa, Big Sky Mind. This is not your personal mind; it is mind itself—

the same mind that is in all of us, the universal mind. It is said that everyone has the same Buddha Nature. Your Buddha Nature is as good as anyone else's. It is not based on cleverness, or any other distinguishing characteristics; it is the same Buddha Nature in all things.

As close as this meditative awareness is, it is still out of grasp without some effort of quieting the everyday monkey mind. As simple as it sounds to simply follow the breath and count to ten without thinking of other things, experience shows that this is no small task. Such is the nature of our ordinary mind, and without disciplining our attention, our awareness will constantly be filled with "I" awareness.

In meditation, we become aware of the impossibility of stopping thoughts, and this is progress. No matter how earnest our intent, thoughts still arise. It is what the mind does; the thoughts are its natural effervescence. Instead of stopping these thoughts, we learn to not follow them. They arise, that's what they do. But we learn to not follow them, analyze them, or pursue them in anyway. The advice is often given to note what is happening by saying "Thinking" in your mind when you notice thoughts arising. Note it and go back to the present breath.

You will come to know the nature of your mind by this practice. You will see how just trying to sit quietly for ten minutes without interruptions from your mind is quite impossible. At first this is a bit aggravating, and it seems like you are constantly saying "Thinking" and how can this be peaceful? But with practice you learn to pay less and less attention to these "mind waves." Where did they come from? Where did they go? You begin to see how insubstantial these thoughts are, and you pull your attention to a deeper place wherein you are neither disturbed nor distracted by these demanding thoughts.

There are numerous meditation styles in Buddhism, some involving very elaborate visualizations, and others having a much simpler object of meditational focus, like the breath. We will explore *vipassana* style in depth, as it is representative of the core meditational practice throughout Buddhism.

How long you do this is not as important as simply doing it. If you only have a few minutes, five or ten minutes, do it anyway. Eventually you might build up to twenty minutes, but don't force that on yourself at the start.

Sit with your spine straight. If you can sit in lotus or half-lotus posture, fine, but even sitting in a chair with your feet flat on the floor will do. Bring your head and spine into alignment with your ears over your shoulders, as if your head were being gently pulled from above. You can let your hands rest naturally on your lap, palms up to receive; or alternately you could have your palms down resting on your thighs if you feel the need for grounding; or you could hold your hands in what's called "the cosmic mudra." Form the mudra by letting your hands drop to your lap, close to your body with palms up. Slide your right hand under the left, both palms still up, so the fingers of your left hand cover the fingers of your right. Bring your thumbs up a few inches from your palms and let them lightly touch together, as if you were forming an oval with your hands (see figure on page 32).

You can close your eyes or keep them half open, blankly looking at a spot on the floor four feet in front of you. Relax your jaw and mouth muscles so you can breathe through your mouth and nose with ease. Placing your tongue on the roof of your mouth can help relax your jaw.

Steady your breath and deepen it in a controlled, yet not forced, manner. Now simply keep your attention on the breath for the duration of the meditation. As a meditational focus, say to yourself "Breathing in" on the in-breath and "Breathing out" on the out-breath. This helps pull your attention back to the moment when your mind begins to wander. Notice the subtle rising on the in-breath and the subtle falling on the out-breath. When thoughts arise—and they will—simply notice them, but don't follow them, and return your attention to the breath. Follow your breath by naming it "Breathing in, breathing out." Take special notice of the gaps between thoughts and experience the spaciousness.

Be gentle with yourself and try not to judge your experience. Just be with the experience. When your mind wanders, just gently pull your attention back to the breath. Whatever arises, just note it, but don't analyze it. Picture your thoughts of having

Figure 1. BASIC MEDITATION POSTURE. *Inset*: COSMIC MUDRA.

nothing to attach to, like champagne bubbles in a glass, rising, and then gone.

With time, you learn to touch this practice lightly with your attention, allowing a far greater portion of your attention to rest in pure observing, emptiness. The advice is sometimes given to focus on the breath with 25 percent of your attention, and with 75 percent simply being open and receptive and observing. The 25 percent is the practice, the 75 percent is the experience. But the 25 percent is also the foundation; it keeps us from simply mind-tripping and calling it meditation.

This practice of focusing on the next breath and letting go of thoughts is most beneficial at other times of the day when you are not meditating. When you are obsessing on a thought or wrestling with some issue throughout the day, your practice in meditation of not following the thoughts really pays off. With practice, you become skilled at dropping the thought and returning to the moment. The benefit that this brings throughout the day cannot be overstated. Perhaps that is why meditation is called "practice" in Buddhism; in meditation we're practicing a skill that will be called on throughout the day.

As an example, many of us have certain activities that we engage in that always seem to trigger our issues. It's not unusual that arduous activities, like tedious chores, trigger tape loop scenarios of the events of one's life. This is when we are particularly prone to buried anger and resentment issues that seem to demand our attention. There is a mild benefit from this experience—the adrenaline released from the anger gets translated into getting the job done that's in front of you. The downside is that this is altogether negative energy, and takes you totally out of the present moment. This is when the practice of letting go of issues as they arise, developed on the meditation cushion, is of real value in the everyday life. Ah! Breaking the grip of these incessant issues is true freedom.

Walking Meditation

Once the basic technique is learned, it can be applied in endless variations. Walking meditation is another popular form and is particularly helpful for those who have difficulty sitting. As with sitting meditation, the intent is to become more mindful of the moment and not let our thoughts wander aimlessly. Thich Nhat Hanh has done much to promote Buddhism and meditation in the West. In his numerous books, such as *Being Peace* and *Peace is Every Step,* Thich Nhat Hanh encourages us to incorporate meditation techniques throughout the day, whether we are walking, driving, cooking, eating, etc. We can practice focusing on our breath and becoming conscious of the moment. Hanh has written numerous little sayings that can be incorporated into our meditations, such as "Breathing in, I calm my body, breathing out, I smile." This could be incorporated in your walking meditation.

Try it and you will see, by direct experience, the impact of smiling on your general well-being.

With walking meditation, we are not walking to get somewhere; we want to learn to be with the walking experience. It is good to slow down your pace and synchronize your steps with your breath. You might breathe in for two, three, or four steps, and do the same with your out-breath. Find your natural rhythm. When thoughts arise, dismiss them just as you would with sitting meditation and return to the breath and the moment.

Become conscious of your connection to the earth. Feel her beneath your feet. Add sacredness to your walk by becoming thankful for the earth and her beauty on the in-breath and send blessings to the earth and her creatures on the out-breath. You can slow down your pace and note the separate sensations of walking itself. Note the sensations of lifting your foot, moving it forward, placing it down and shifting your weight forward. Be present with all aspects of your experience.

Gardening Meditation

From meditation we learn to become mindful with all of our activities. Even activities aimed at doing something are opportunities to practice mindfulness. Gardening is particularly favorable for this. As with sitting and walking meditations, we establish the intent of not letting the mind wander, and use our breath to bring us back to the moment. Stand back from the garden and observe it and listen to it while you are practicing standing meditation. Be willing to be the garden's servant, tending to its needs. What activity are you drawn to while simply observing the garden with openness? Weeding, planting, thinning, pruning, cultivating, watering? What calls out to you?

As you approach the activity you are drawn to, stay in your mindfulness practice. Tend to the breath, dismiss thoughts and surrender to the needs of the situation in front of you. Try not to willfully do the activity, as if you were imposing yourself on the situation. Instead, form a relationship with the activity; let it be done *through* you. Let the plants and the garden inform you what needs to be done. Trust that if you surrender to the needs, the skills will be pulled out of you to meet those needs. Gardening in this way can be a wonderful affirmation of the interconnectedness of all life.

Death and Rebirth

Buddhism looks death squarely in the eye and says, "Deal with it." At first, this is hard to embrace, and then liberating for us Westerners who have been given a rather morbid view of death. By not wanting to look at it, we treat death as if it were a shock, with an attitude of "How could this have happened?" Buddhists are realists; it *is* going to happen, better to deal with it consciously than to let it sneak up on you. Since death is assured, why not prepare for it?

Reincarnation, or more accurately, rebirth, is a central teaching in Buddhism. With an understanding that the soul will be reborn into another incarnation, carrying with it the lessons and karma from previous incarnations, Buddhists give a great deal of attention to the circumstances surrounding death. There is the belief that we can influence future incarnations for a more favorable rebirth by living in alignment with the Buddha's teachings in this life. Our karma comes with us into the next incarnation and directly influences the nature of our rebirth.

Moreover, it is taught that one can learn to navigate in the space between lives, called the *bardos,* to also more favorably influence the nature of one's rebirth. It is said to be a great blessing to die with loved ones and other practitioners creating a positive environment and atmosphere for making this huge transition. To die in the presence of loved ones involved in their spiritual practices creates an atmosphere that can facilitate the transition.

Teachings from the Bardos

The Tibetan Book of the Dead delineates the experience of the soul's journey from death to rebirth. The *bardos* are the specific transition states the soul will experience before rebirth. There are bardos related to states of consciousness for the living as well, but here we will be focusing on the bardos of dying. By meditating on these states of consciousness of dying, practitioners are practicing for when they will be asked to do this in the bardo states without the grounding of the body. Unbounded mind might sound delightful, but it can be a wild ride! Anything you think about manifests—great if you are in a good place, not so great if you're not. Negative thoughts can create their own reality in the bardos, so practitioners learn how to center themselves, even in the face of death.

Bardos: *Transition states; or, more specifically, the state in-between births.*

The typical duration in the bardos is said to be forty-nine days, the first twenty-one completing karma from this life, and the last twenty-eight days the soul is already more involved with moving toward its next rebirth. Sogyale Rinpoche, in *The Tibetan Book of Living and Dying,* says that the soul is seven times more clairvoyant in the bardo states than in living states. The bardo states are considered a major opportunity for enlightenment for advanced practitioners, and a major opportunity to influence the nature of their rebirth.

It is taught that during the dying person's stay in the bardo states, our prayers, best wishes, and meditations have an extremely influential impact on helping the soul move toward a favorable rebirth. Since the soul is seven times more clairvoyant, you don't even have to say your prayers; your thoughts will be felt. In Tibet, *The Tibetan Book of the Dead* is read aloud by family members daily to provide guidance while the soul is in the bardo states.

How can we use this information? First of all, by being more conscious and reverent in honoring someone's death. Know beyond a doubt that your prayers are being helpful. Even holding the person's image in your heart with loving-kindness does immeasurable benefit. Particularly in the first twenty-one days while the soul is still attached to issues of this life. The same day of the week that the person died, and more specifically the same hour and place, are said to be particularly favorable times for connecting with the departing soul.

Of course this teaching carries a warning, or at least a caution. Since the soul is still susceptible to the thoughts and emotions of loved ones, we would be doing a tremendous disservice to the soul by harboring resentments, thinking negative thoughts, or squabbling over possessions. Our negative thoughts and actions can cause a response by the soul in the bardos, deflecting its true course. When we realize the karmic implications of the backside of this teaching, we see how important it is to put our best spiritual foot forward and do what we can do to assist and honor the soul's journey through the bardos.

The impact of this direct and sacred approach to death on us Westerners is profound. Perhaps it is time that death comes "out of the closet," just as birth came out of the closet in the '60s, when women were demanding that birth not be treated like a medical crisis; it is now time for death to be embraced and brought into a healthier understanding in our culture. When a dying person is surrounded only by panic, grief, and suffering, this does not support the experience and creates a shock. Imagine a departing soul sensing all the grief and sorrow it is causing for loved ones merely by dying. This shock, and accompanying guilt, can cause attachment to the death experience, making it difficult for the departing soul to successfully navigate the bardos in between lives.

It is taught that to best support a dying person's experience, one can be involved in personal spiritual practice in the presence of the dying person. This will help the dying person attune to the highest within himself. Picturing the dying person's consciousness dissolving into the light is said to be very supportive and helpful for the departing soul. Grief is going to be there, personal loss is real, but also introducing these sacred practices into our experiences with death can help bring us into a higher awareness of what is going on, and also support the dying person in a helpful way.

Too often, those dying are left alone in their experience, as many believe one should not talk about death to a dying person. Better to cheer them up and help them think about something positive. Paradoxically, this is the one thing that is most occupying their minds, and yet, the one thing no one will talk about! We can do a great service for the dying by allowing them to speak of their experience. You do not need great words of wisdom, simply listen with a compassionate heart.

Tonglen

In Tibetan Buddhism there is the teaching of *Tonglen.* It is the inverse of the practice of breathing in light and breathing out darkness. With Tonglen, you breathe in the suffering, darkness, and pain of others, feel it dissolve in shunyata, and breathe out light, love, and a compassionate wish that others may be free of suffering. You first picture the other person as another you. You essentially empathize to such a degree that you can feel within yourself the emotions of the dying person. Then with shunyata, you picture these emotions dissolving in the emptiness, and you send back love. Tonglen is a beautiful practice to engage in when being with a dying person. It allows you to be fully present with the person in the truth of their experience, while simultaneously doing them a tremendous service.

Grieving the loss of a loved one is natural and healthy. But it is advised we grieve in private, and then, when we are with a dying person, realize the sacredness of the moment and attend to it. Realize the tremendous impact you can have on the experience by staying in your center and your heart. Even if others around you are in their grief and panic, you can do tremendous good by silently doing your Tonglen practice. Helping to create a peaceful atmosphere, you become like a tuning fork for the dying person to align with. Embrace the eternal nature of the dying person's soul—the soul is not dying—simply shedding a tired body it no longer needs.

Tonglen: *Exchanging oneself for another. Feeling directly the sufferings and pains of another. Breathing in this pain as if it were one's own, and dissolving it in the compassionate heart, then breathing out the compassionate wish of liberation from others' suffering.*

The Buddha's teachings are based on the understanding that attaching to anything temporal creates ultimate suffering. Attend to the eternal. The body is temporal. For you, for me, for our children's children's children, death of the body will happen. But the Buddha Nature is eternal. Relate to the Buddha Nature of the dying person and you become like a beacon in the night, creating a pathway for the dying person to find his or her way home.

There is a Tibetan practice, called *phowa,* of ejecting the consciousness into the nature mind while in the bardos. Only an advanced practitioner of the meditational practices would be able to do this. However, it is taught that if those surrounding the dying person are practicing phowa meditation, visualizing the dying person dissolving into light, the oneness, then their efforts are said to greatly benefit the dying person's transition through the bardos.

Another ramification of the Buddhist teachings on dying for the Western seeker deals with the question of how our lives come about. In the emerging Western spiritual movement, it is common to believe that you chose this life, you chose your parents, and so on. This is an interesting eruption of spontaneous spiritual consciousness. I don't believe this can be traced to a specific teacher or tradition; it just seems to have emerged. This view has a healthy component in that it fosters taking responsibility for the life you are living—this life is not a fluke, nor a mistake; there is intent behind it. However, this "you chose this life" view implies a discontinuity of lives. One can imagine a soul thumbing through a catalog and selecting a particular life, implying there could be a randomness of lives, a sampling of this one, that one, and then another.

In contrast, the Buddhist teachings suggest a *continuity* of lives; basically, we pick up where we left off. It is then apparent that it is in *this* life that we make the choices that will lead to our next rebirth. Our earthly lives exist on the plane of reality where choice is possible. In the bardo states, in between lives, there isn't an individual consciousness that could make choices, only the imprints on your energy field from previous choices you've made. In-between lives is too late. The karma of our past choices will already be pulling us into the next incarnation that perfectly fits the karma we have created. It is in this life, now, today, that we are making the choices that will influence our next rebirth. In this light, it follows that it is advisable to start today by accepting the lessons of our current life and begin living in such a way that will lead to a favorable rebirth.

Bodhisattvas

Bodhisattvas have dedicated themselves to the uplifting of all sentient beings, and vowed to return incarnation after incarnation, until all are free. The Bodhisattva vow reveals the path:

> Sentient beings are numberless: I vow to liberate them.
> Delusions are inexhaustible: I vow to transcend them.
> Dharma teachings are boundless: I vow to master them.
> The Buddha's enlightened way is unsurpassable: I vow to embody it.

The Bodhisattva path sets a spiritual high-water mark. Few of us have it in us to dedicate our entire life to uplifting humanity, but we could all benefit by moving in that direction. Draw on the community of Bodhisattvas on our planet when you need spiritual strength. There are times when each of us gets tested in life, times when

Bodhisattva: ***One who has forsaken his own individual enlightenment in favor of working on the release of all beings from suffering.***

the high road is clear, but we lack the spiritual strength to overcome the tendencies of the past. This is when you can draw on the community strength of the Bodhisattvas. Invoke the vow and you align with the collective strength of all dedicated seekers the world over, past and present, doing what they can to bring sacred awareness to our planet. We don't evolve alone. The work that others do to live a more conscious life benefits you; your attempts to live more mindfully spread out and assist others on their path.

Compassion and Tonglen Practice

Perhaps the greatest gift Buddhism has to offer the modern world is the teachings of compassion. Buddhism teaches the interconnectedness of all life. We are all here together, and if there is suffering going on somewhere on the planet, we will all feel this at some level. Thus, compassion for self, others, plants, animals, and minerals is a central teaching of the Buddhist path. Compassion in and of itself is a noble principle, but we must have tools for processing the compassion, or we will get pulled into the suffering ourselves.

The practice of Tonglen is the revolutionary concept that Buddhism has developed to deal with compassion so you are not simply *carrying* the suffering of others. We discussed Tonglen in the section on death, but its applications are not limited to this arena; all suffering, pain, anger, and negative karma can be dissolved with this practice.

First, sit quietly and focus on awakening your own Bodhichitta. Ask for assistance from all the Buddhas and Bodhisattvas to awaken your heart/mind to compassion and loving-kindness. Once you feel this love and compassion, imagine someone you know who is going through a difficult time. Imagine the other person's pain and suffering as a dark cloud of negative energy. Now breathe this dark, smoky pain into yourself and imagine that you have taken on all of the suffering of your friend. Sogyal Rinpoche, in *The Tibetan Book of Living and Dying,* says that this can help break our patterns of self-cherishing and remove our personal negative karma. Feel this dark cloud of suffering move right through you, as if you were a Hollywood storefront and behind you is nothing but empty space. In this way, there is no place within you for the darkness to take hold and attach. After you have dissolved the darkness, reconnect to your heart of loving-kindness and send forth this love, light, and compassion to your friend, picturing all of the darkness that was previously there being replaced by this radiant light. Continue this process until you feel in your heart that your friend's well-being has been restored.

Next, extend your practice to all beings who might be going through a similar difficulty in their lives. Imagine the millions of people the world over who must be going through a similar suffering at this very moment. Breathe in all their pain and feel it. Dissolve it into the void of empty space, and then send out the compassionate wish that all beings may be free of suffering.

After practicing Tonglen for some time, you begin to realize that we are all individual harbors on the same ocean of collective emotion. It is futile to attempt to keep your personal harbor clean until you realize the source is the ocean, and begin the practice of helping to clean the collective ocean of emotion.

We are all interconnected, thus practicing Tonglen gives you a technique for dealing with this inescapable reality. We can't hide from the suffering of others and we can't push it away without it affecting us in some way. But we can open our hearts and begin the process of healing each other, alleviating the pain in the world, and thus, heal ourselves as well.

After Thoughts

"Anger and hatred are our real enemies. These are the forces we most need to confront and defeat, not the temporary 'enemies' who appear intermittently throughout life."[5]

—The Dalai Lama

"In the beginner's mind there are many possibilities, but in the expert's there are few."[6]

—Shunryu Suzuki

"A day spent judging another is a painful day. A day spent judging yourself is a painful day. You don't have to believe your judgments; they're simply an old habit."[7]

—Jack Kornfield

"This is my simple religion: There is no need for temples; no need for complicated philosophy. Our own brain, our own heart is our temple; the philosophy is kindness."[8]

—The Dalai Lama

Suggested Reading

Bancroft, Anne. *The Dhammapada.* Rockport, Mass.: Element, 1997.

Beck, Charlotte Joko. *Everyday Zen.* New York, N.Y.: HarperSanFrancisco, 1989.

Chadwick, David. *The Crooked Cucumber: The Life and Zen Teachings of Shunryu Suzuki.* New York, N.Y.: Broadway Books, 1999.

Chödrön, Pema. *When Things Fall Apart.* Boston & London: Shambhala, 1997.

———. *Start Where You Are.* Boston & London: Shambhala, 1994.

Dalai Lama XIV. Translated by Geshe Thupten Jinpa. *The Power of Compassion.* San Francisco, Calif.: Thorsons, 1995.

———. *Awakening the Mind, Lightening the Heart.* New York, N.Y.: HarperSanFrancisco, 1995.

———. *Tibetan Portrait.* New York, N.Y.: Rizzoli International Publications, 1996.

Lama Surya Das. *Awakening the Buddha Within*. New York, N.Y.: Broadway Books, 1997.

Hanh, Thich Nhat. *The Heart of Buddha's Teachings*. Berkeley, Calif.: Parallax Press, 1998.

———. *Peace Is Every Step*. New York, N.Y.: Bantam Books, 1991.

———. *Being Peace*. Berkeley, Calif.: Parallax Press, 1987.

Kohn, Sherab Chödzin. *The Awakened One: A Life of the Buddha*. Boston: Shambhala, 1994.

Kornfield, Jack. *A Path With Heart*. New York, N.Y.: Bantam Doubleday Dell, 1993.

———. *After the Ecstacy, the Laundry*. New York, N.Y.: Bantam Doubleday Dell, 2001.

Norbu, Namkhai. *The Crystal and the Way of Light*. New York, N.Y.: Arkana, 1993. (First published by Routledge and Kegan Paul Ltd., 1986.)

Rinpoche, Sogyal. *The Tibetan Book of Living and Dying*. New York, N.Y.: HarperSanFrancisco: 1994.

Reps, Paul, and Nyogen Sensaki. *Zen Flesh, Zen Bones*. Tokyo: Tuttle Publishing, 1957.

Salzberg, Sharon. *Voices of Insight*. Boston & London: Shambhala, 1999.

———. *Loving Kindness*. Boston & London: Shambhala, 1995.

Schneider, David. *Street Zen*. Boston & London: Shambhala, 1993.

Smith, Huston. *World's Religions*. New York, N.Y.: HarperSanFrancisco, 1958.

Suzuki, D.T. *Essays in Zen Buddhism*. New York, N.Y.: Grove Press, Inc., 1949.

Suzuki, Shunryu. *Zen Mind, Beginner's Mind*. New York, N.Y.: Weatherhill, 1970.

Trungpa, Chögyam. *Cutting Through Spiritual Materialism.* Boston & London: Shambhala, 1973.

———. *Training the Mind.* Boston & London: Shambhala, 1993.

———. *Shambhala: The Sacred Path of the Warrior.* Boston & London: Shambhala, 1984.

Endnotes

1. Lama Surya Das. *Awakening the Buddha Within.* p. 19.
2. Huston Smith. *World's Religions.* p. 71.
3. Anne Bancroft. *The Dhammapada.* p. 35.
4. Shunryu Suzuki. *Zen Mind, Beginner's Mind.* p. 35.
5. The Dalai Lama. *Tibetan Portrait.* p. 30.
6. Shunryu Suzuki. *Zen Mind, Beginner's Mind.* p. 21.
7. Jack Kornfield. *Buddha's Little Instruction Book.* p. 108.
8. The Dalai Lama. *Tibetan Portrait,* p. 72.

HINDUISM

Let your aim be one and single;
Let your hearts be joined in one—
The mind at rest in unison—
At peace with all, so may you be.[1]

Hymns from the Rig-Veda
trans. by Jean Le Mee

THIS IS THE simple truth spawning the vast complexity that is Hinduism: God is in all things, including the self. From this simple truth an incredibly diverse and complex maze arises, because the Hindu system allows for and acknowledges that there are many paths to God. Upon first entering these teachings, the Western seeker can feel overwhelmed by the wide panorama of gods, goddesses, beliefs, and practices. However, this complexity has a basis in simplicity as a saying from Hinduism reveals: "There is but one truth, although it will be given many names." This completely captures the spirit of Hinduism—there are many paths to the same truth.

One of the beautiful qualities of Hinduism is that it does offer different paths for different people, so to know Hinduism, you needn't know all the various paths. Experience it through the lens that you are most drawn to; this will get you to the essence. Since all of the various paths, yogas, teachings, gods and goddess of Hinduism lead to the same source, I would encourage you to first read through the whole chapter, and then zero in on the material that most appeals to you.

Hinduism is amorphous, evolving, and hard to pinpoint. Approaching Hinduism after Buddhism makes the Buddhist path seem almost stark in comparison. Buddha taught to focus on that which you could know and control—your mind and behavior specifically. In contrast, Hinduism embraces the mystical aspect of life, that which cannot be known by the mind. Many spiritual teachings and teachers that have come to us from the East have their roots in Hinduism. By poring over the teachings, you become familiar with the soil from which these illumined souls have drawn their inspiration. Hinduism is filled with the stories of saints, sages, and holy ones who have had this experience of Divine union. Although the techniques for experiencing the transcendent state are many and varied, we will see that there are a few unifying principles that all Hindus embrace.

Rather than presenting an objective scholarly account of Hinduism (other authors have done this admirably and are presented in the suggested reading list, see page 112), in this chapter we will explore the material by delving into the various practices of Hinduism. In this way, we will weave the teachings throughout the chapter where they are applicable. First we will explore a broad overview and then delve into the material.

An Overview of Hinduism

Hinduism is the oldest of the world's religions, with its roots going back before recorded history. All of the Eastern religions can trace their roots to Hinduism. The belief that all individual souls will eventually reunite with Brahman (God) is a common denominator that links the many schools of Hinduism. This reuniting with God is called *moksha,* which translates as "liberation from worldly existence." Although all Hindus share the same goal of moksha, the paths to get there are many and varied.

Moksha: ***Absolute liberation. Union with the Divine and freedom from all worldly attachments.***

Even though everyone will eventually attain moksha, this takes lifetimes, thus reincarnation is a cornerstone of Hindu teachings. Reincarnation is not, however, a random sampling of lives. Through the principle of *karma,* lessons learned and not learned, are carried over from lifetime to lifetime in the soul's memory. Essentially, you pick up in this life where you left off in your past life. To extend this forward, it is through your choices of action in this life that you lay the groundwork for your next life.

Karma: ***Essentially, you pick up in this life where you left off in your last life.***

Hinduism is pervasive. Imagine a culture that for thousands of years has honored the spiritual aspirant as its hero. Hinduism isn't just seen as an adjunct to life by its adherents; it *is* life. More than any of the world's other religions, Hinduism allows for and encourages individual differences, and even offers different spiritual paths according to these differences. Not only in broad, sweeping terms that each must find their own path, but also in specifically mapping out the distinguishing traits of personality types and offering a unique form of worship for different temperaments.

In the West, we are familiar with yoga as body postures and stretching, called Hātha Yoga, but this is only one of the yoga paths. *Yoga* means "union," specifically, "union with God." There is also Jnana Yoga ("the path of knowledge"), Bhakti Yoga ("the path of devotion"), Karma Yoga ("the path of service") and Raja Yoga ("the path of action," including Hatha Yoga). Each of these paths are suitable means of attaining moksha, and one is encouraged to find the path that most suits one's natural inclinations.

Before we further explore the various paths of Hinduism, let's first explore the basic cosmology—it is hard to tell the players without a program.

The Hindu Cosmology

Hinduism is very unique in its view of God. First, there is a distinction between two levels of God. There is God with qualities and attributes *(Saguna)*, and there is God without any distinguishing features *(Nirguna)*. God without attributes is Brahman. Brahman is all-inclusive and all-embracing, without limits or characteristics. Anything that could be conceived or described could not be Brahman, because that would limit by definition, and Brahman is without limits. This level of God is seen as a vast emptiness, from which all creation arises (see chart below).

Brahman

Nirguna (God without attributes)

Atman

Saguna (God with attributes)

Brahma (The Creator)	***Vishnu*** (The Preserver)	***Shiva*** (The Destroyer)
Sarasvati	***Lakshmi***	***Shakti***
	Rama and Krishna	***Uma, Kali, Durga, Mahadeva***

Brahman is both transcendent and imminent; both beyond creation and within creation. There is no separation between the creator and the created. The creator is infused within the created. This allows for a reverence for all forms of life—it's all God. Hinduism doesn't have a fall from grace, the Divine is ever-present and within as well as without.

Brahman cannot be known, but can be experienced. Although without attributes, the phrase "*sat-chit-ananda*" points us toward it: absolute existence, absolute consciousness, and absolute bliss. The life stories of Ramana Maharshi, Yogananda, and Sri Ramakrishna are but a few examples of individuals who have lived and sustained this level of consciousness. You can find books about them listed at the end of this chapter.

Atman

There is a subtlety within the understanding of Brahman that allows for the human experience. Atman is that aspect of Brahman that relates to the human realm. It is as if there are *layers* of Brahman, some dealing with realities beyond the human realm, and Atman is another layer of this Supreme Reality relating specifically to human existence. It is the one Atman that underlies all human consciousness. The subtlety is that Atman and Brahman are considered one, not different nor separate.

To align with Atman within is to align with the part of you that is eternal and has never been wounded or tainted by life's experiences. It is the place within you that witnesses the experiences of life. All of the various paths we will explore lead to aligning with this eternal part of your being.

Although all Hindus see Brahman as the eternal Supreme Reality, it is hard to worship something that has no form whatsoever. Thus, Hinduism also allows for personal gods with specific attributes with whom one can love, cherish, seek guidance from, and form a personal relationship. This allows for an incredibly rich pantheon of deities who are acceptable for worship. This myriad of gods and goddesses being worshiped are not viewed as being rivals with one another . . . there is room to allow others their god of choice, with a knowing that all of these gods are expressions of the same Absolute God, Brahman, beyond the human potential to identify.

One can imagine the attitude of, "Since it is all an illusion anyway, your illusion of God is as good as mine, and mine is as good as yours." The tolerance for other each other's gods is extended to other religions, at least in principle. Even within the same family, there may be members who worship different deities without judgment of each other. The beauty of this is self-evident.

On a trip to Bali, a predominantly Hindu island in Indonesia, a cab driver told us that it was against the law to attempt to convert anybody to your religious views on Bali. If a person has a religion, honor it. If a person doesn't have a religion or is seeking, then of course it is permissible to share your beliefs, otherwise no attempts to convert others from his or her existing beliefs is allowed. This is a great contribution to global spirituality. This path of honoring another person's path to God seems to be a welcome salve to the wounds that separate religions.

Studying Hinduism puts religious arguments in an interesting light. Rational arguments about religion miss the point. It is not meant to be rational. Hinduism shows us that religion is a means of worship; *that's* the point. Worship is what it is all about, not whether it is rational or not; not if it is better than another form of worship or not.

> ***The act of worship activates centers of consciousness that cannot be attained, nor understood, by the rational mind.***

The Personal Gods: Brahma, Vishnu, and Shiva

The trinity of Brahma (the Creator), Vishnu (the Preserver), and Shiva (the Destroyer) are the main division of Saguna—God with attributes. Here we see the different manifestations of the Divine, in its creating, nurturing, and transforming ways. Hinduism is magnificent in taking account of and allowing for different temperaments. It is taught that you should follow your natural temperament in aligning with the God of your choice. It's not like trying to worship one God or another. It is more like searching until one speaks to you. Nor is strict allegiance to any God required.

Shiva may be the deity that most speaks to you, but there may be times you are drawn to worship Vishnu, and so forth.

This trinity of Brahma, Vishnu, and Shiva is considered archetypal and passive; the ground from which creation springs. Each of these gods needs an activating agent, a consort, to manifest his qualities. Thus there are goddesses and even human deities associated with each of the gods that help bring their latent quality into manifestation.

Although Hindu art and iconography may seem cartoonlike with its surrealistic presentation of "Blue Gods" with "many arms," and so forth, the way each of these gods is portrayed is significant to the detail. In Hindu art, gods are always indicated by having four or more arms; humans with two. Blue represents the highest spiritual qualities. Each of the items the deities hold in their hands is indicative of his qualities. Even body posture and what the god is standing or sitting on has relevance.

Brahma: The Creator. Portrayed as having four heads, looking in the four directions, from which he gathers and spreads wisdom. Brahma is the wisdom and intelligence behind all of creation. Brahma's consort is the goddess Sarasvati, the goddess of speech and intelligence, and she is the patron of the arts. In the evolving nature of Hinduism, Brahma has been demoted from a once-prominent position in the Hindu religion to now being acknowledged as part of the trinity, but rarely worshipped.

The question arises as to why the Creator God would no longer be worshipped? The answer seems to be redundancy. As the other two gods, Vishnu and Shiva, have grown in popularity, their feminine consorts also are seen as the creative life-giving aspect of God, and thus Brahma has become redundant.

Vishnu: The Preserver, who represents the sustaining and nurturing qualities of God. His wife, or consort, is Lakshmi. God creates, and God protects and nurtures, and God destroys and takes away. Vishnu is the protective qualities of God and is widely worshipped throughout the Hindu world.

Vishnu holds the conch shell, representing creation with its ability to emulate the sacred sound *OM*, from which all creation arises; a discus representing the universal mind, with its ability to illuminate and also cut through ignorance; a mace representing his power and authority; and the lotus flower representing the eternal beauty that springs forth from the mud of reality.

Those of the Bhakti path of devotional love often align with Vishnu. Rama and Krishna are said to be human incarnations of Vishnu, and to worship them is to worship Vishnu.

Vishnu's consort, Lakshmi, represents wealth and fortune and is also seen as the perfect wife. Whenever humanity is out of balance, Vishnu incarnates in human form as an avatar and Lakshmi incarnates at the same time as his wife. When Vishnu incarnated as Rama, Lakshmi became his lover, Sita (as told in the Ramayana, to be discussed later). When Vishnu incarnated as Krishna, Lakshmi was there as Radha and later Rukmini (as told in the Puranas, to be discussed later).

Shiva: The Destroyer is a fierce title, but Shiva is much loved and worshiped. Not as much as Shiva himself, but with his Divine consort, Shakti, the Universal Divine mother known by many names: Parvati, Uma, Mahadevi, Durga, and Kali to name a few. The principles of all the gods are held within Shiva. In one hand is his drum, which beats the rhythm of the universe and establishes the cycles of time. All that comes into form eventually sheds form by his decree in the cyclic dance of time. He holds the flame, symbolizing eternal truth and the transformation of the mind when burned free from an ego-centered view of life and aligned with the transcendent teachings. Another of his hands points upward in the symbol of a blessing. This is the preserver aspect of the trinity being expressed through Shiva. His remaining hand crosses his body and points downward, like the trunk of an elephant. This references Ganesha, son of Shiva, the four-armed elephant god. Ganesha is the remover of obstacles, and is much loved by Hindus. Shiva is seen with one leg raised, as if dancing, and the other leg standing on the child of ignorance, which he ruthlessly stamps out. Known as "Lord of the Dance," the raised leg suggests the feminine expression of Shiva, Shakti, dancing life to a higher level.

Shakti is the feminine expression of Shiva and represents the universal life force, *prana*. The Tantra and Kundalini schools of Hinduism are particularly aligned with her. Shakti awakens the latent kundalini energy and causes it to rise to the full flowering of human potential and communion with God. This will be discussed further in the section on the chakras, page 91.

Prana: *The universal life force sustaining all of life—the breath of life.*

Origins of Hinduism

Hinduism is ancient. The Vedas, the sacred scriptures that are the foundation of Hinduism, are the oldest spiritual writings in the world. Where Buddhism and Christianity can be traced to a specific person and time in history, Hinduism has no such direct lineage and draws from many sources. The Aryans, who settled into northwest India from Iran and Afghanistan approximately 1,600 B.C.E., were a dominant influence. Dates have been disputed between Western and Hindu sources. Be that as it may, early dates must be viewed as approximate.

Many sources cite the beginning of Hinduism with these Aryan settlers. Others sources dispute this claim, believing that the Arayans were also influenced by the indigenous beliefs of the prevailing culture of the time, and the emergence of Hinduism was the blending of the two cultures. Since these teachings did not emerge in the homelands of Afghanistan and the Iran of the Aryans, the argument that it was somehow imported is weakened.

Hindus themselves do not trace their origin to a specific group of people, instead seeing their teachings as from the *Sanatana Dharma,* or eternal truth, the name they give to their religion. The Sanatana Dharma has always been there. Hindu legend places the origin of the Vedas much earlier than Western dating. It is believed that as humanity entered into a Dark Age, approximately 3,000 B.C.E., the sacred hymns and practices that had been part of the culture since the dawn of time, transmitted orally from one generation to the next, were gathered together and written down to preserve the teachings.

Core Beliefs of Hinduism

Although its branches are many, there are a few core beliefs central to all who practice Hinduism. Namely, reincarnation, along with the principle of karma; the belief that moksha, liberation from the wheel of death and rebirth, is inherent in all beings; that the path to moksha is through purifying the self of ego and bodily attachments; and a final common denominator is the distinction between what is real and not real. Hindus look at the physical material world as not real—illusionary—while the only real realm is the Supreme Reality, Brahman, beyond all labels and definitions.

It is taught that it is within each soul to eventually reach complete union with the Supreme Reality and become free from rebirth. Moksha, ultimate liberation, is the goal of all Hindus. Until then, an individual soul will reincarnate life after life, bound by the laws of karma, slowly awakening and learning life's lessons.

The Western scriptures teach a strong distinction between good and evil. In Hinduism, there is no evil; there is a place for the dark forces to work as catalysts in the ultimate development of consciousness. Instead of teaching that good can overcome evil, it taught that maintaining equilibrium, by creating a balance between the light and dark forces, is the way. The Hindu scriptures ultimately tie together all aspects of life and death, rather than dividing the world into good and bad.

While in Bali, we noticed that the statues in temples were always clothed with a black-and-white checkered sarong around their waists. We were informed that this was to keep the awareness of light and dark forces in balance. Shopkeepers placed offerings of incense and rice on the sidewalk in front of their stores to appease and honor the dark forces, and a separate offering inside the store to the gods—best to keep them both happy—live in harmony with both by honoring and acknowledging both the light and the dark.

Stages of Life

Hinduism identifies four distinct stages in a person's spiritual life.

The Student Stage: This is the time in life to be supported by family and culture in order to pursue the training and education needed to meet one's own obligations. It is considered a gathering phase, where one is meant to gather the energy, experiences, and training necessary for one's future life.

The Householder Stage: This is the time in life to have a family and surrender to all of the responsibilities and roles it entails. It is considered spiritual service to provide for the needs of one's family and community.

The Retirement Stage: Considered to begin around the time of the birth of the first grandchild. One retires from active family and career activities to focus on spiritual development.

The Sannyasin Stage: The stage to renounce all worldly attachments, and center one's attention on God.

These stages start off in a very familiar way to Westerners; the student and householder stages are the same, East or West. However, the Hindu belief that these are important spiritual stages of life is empowering for those in family lives. The family years can be so consuming of one's attention, it would be easy to feel you were missing something by not having the time to devote to spiritual studies. The Hindus teach you can get to the same place through "family yoga." Attend to the needs of those in your family as a blessing, as an offering, as spiritual service. This spiritual service is encouraged to extend to the community, and there is great honor in helping those in need.

Where retirement is the next stage for both the East and the West, its implications are radically different for each. In the West we think of retirement in terms of rest, relaxation, and recreation. In Hinduism, retirement is the time to begin one's spiritual quest in earnest. This is honored as another spiritual initiation, and provides a meaningful direction for this stage in life when many Westerners are going through the "empty nest syndrome," or feeling like life is winding down. The life experiences acquired during the student and householder stages become the fodder that fuels spiritual understanding during the retirement stage.

The West has no reference at all to the final stage, the sannyasin stage. This is the time to completely renounce one's roles and attachments to the material world in absolute surrender to God. This stage, which culminates at a time in life when worldly skills and interests are diminishing, adds honor and integrity to the final stage of life. Those in their householder phase consider it an honor and spiritual merit to be able to support those in the sannyasin phase.

Sannyasin: *One who has renounced worldly roles in favor of completely dedicating life to God.*

When we compare the sannyasin stage with our Western approach to the same stage of life, we can readily see the benefits of their expanded cosmology. This is a time when the outer senses are meant to deteriorate and the inner senses sharpen. We have failed to find a favorable alternative to this stage of growth in the West. At best, we provide comfort and care of the elderly during this time of diminished capacity. The Hindus teach that this is the time for supreme spiritual blossoming. This missing piece in our cosmology explains why we Westerners have such little respect for this stage of life.

What if there was a lifetime of training in preparation for this stage of a winding down of the outer senses, and training for entering into absorption into Divine consciousness? It would make a huge difference in all our lives.

These core principles underlie all of Hinduism, but as we shall see, there are many expressions and paths that spring from these core principles. So, let's begin our search of these paths.

The Bhakti Path of Devotional Love

This is the path of God Realization from the heart. Here, those with a strong emotional nature find solace. Many of the spiritual paths advise quieting the emotions, with the image given of calming the waters of a lake so the surface can reflect in tranquility. Not so on the Bhakti path. The Bhakti path openly embraces the emotional side of life and teaches that through love and devotion, one can come to know God. The forms of expression on the Bhakti path range from ecstatically chanting praises to God, to quiet contemplation on the love of the Divine.

In the West, we picture God the Father, but in the East the Divine is most often experienced as the Mother. It is the Divine Mother who brought potential into manifest form, gives birth to life, and is the recipient of the devotional love of the Divine.

A Bhakti Meditation

A simple way to experience the Bhakti path is to meditate from your heart. While in meditation, sink your attention from the mind and center it on your heart. Visualize Divine love filling your heart and imagine yourself being infused with the qualities of love that you are drawn to, such as joy, compassion, and altruism. Know that the Divine Mother wants to give these qualities to you, as a mother wants to give to her child. Feel your heart growing from this fusion with the Divine Mother. See your heart grow in size until it ultimately fills your entire being. Still see it grow and radiate, engulfing all your awareness. Feel the heart of the Divine Mother beating in your heart. Rest in this love.

This is the Bhakti path. Its simplicity is why it is considered by many sources, including the Bhagavad Gita, as the most direct way to God Realization. Many revered Hindu teachers and saints have taught this path. In *Autobiography of a Yogi,* Yogananda suggests we have a right to demand from the Divine Mother the love we crave, just as a baby demands to be fed from his mother.[2] Sri Ramakrishna is widely regarded as a saint. He was known for going into spontaneous Divine rapture all throughout his life. He demonstrated that one could come to know God through any and all of the world's religions, and he tried them all. Ramakrishna taught that the Bhakti path is the most direct path to God. Ram Dass and his guru Neem Karoli Baba have taught the path of the heart. Ramana Maharshi spent a lifetime in Divine rapport and taught that love was the quality that most described this union. Further information can be found on these great souls in the suggested reading section.

Kirten and Chanting

Kirten is a form of devotional practice currently gaining popularity in the West, and another method for practicing Bhakti Yoga. It is communal singing and chanting praises to God and the holy ones. Its aim is to awaken the emotions of love through chanting and singing to God. Often, a group leader will sing a phrase or two of a song and the audience will sing back the same phrase in unison. Many Hatha Yoga studios in the West are now incorporating kirten and chanting into their offerings. Kirten moistens one's practice and brings you back to the heart.

Kirten and chanting often use the original Sanskrit words. It's easy to feel left out if you don't know the meanings of the foreign words. But here is the beauty of Sanskrit. It is an *intentional* language. The sound of the words triggers the appropriate physiological, emotional, and spiritual responses—you get the meaning at many levels just from the vibrational influences of the vocalized word.

Japa and Mantras

The practice of *japa,* which is repeating the name of God over and over again, is another method for invoking God's love. Saying the name of God as a chant, in any language, is one of the most powerful techniques for dispelling fear and negative thoughts. It is taught that this can be done audibly, silently, with just the lips moving, or within one's self. It is more powerful to practice japa silently, but also more difficult to tame the mind at the same time.

Chanting a mantra is also a direct path. A mantra is a phrase uttered over and over again, audibly or inwardly, as a meditational focus. Using a mantra is a technique for liberating the mind from its negative tendencies. Chanting "OM," sometimes spelled AUM, is an example. Chanting this sacred sound opens one up to higher-level spiritual vibrations—the sound of Brahman.

Contemplating the symbol is also used to heighten one's vibrations. The symbol is made up of three curves and a crescent holding a dot. The lowest curve relates to everyday waking consciousness. The middle curve relates to the subjective imaginative state of consciousness including daydreams and night dreams. The upper curve relates to dreamless sleep, the causal body, and the "other reality" beyond manifestation.

Figure 2. OM SYMBOL.

The crescent relates to the true self beyond apparent form and the dot, *Turiya,* separated from the rest of the symbol by the crescent, shows a separate level of reality, the oneness behind it all, Brahman.

Other popular mantras are: "OM GURU, OM NIMAH SHIVAYA" (OM, blessings to Shiva) and "OM MANI PADME HUM" (OM, jewel of the lotus blossom).

Evolving Hinduism

With the Bhakti movement we see the evolving nature of Hinduism. It is not static; gods come in and out of popularity and change what they represent. The worship of Krishna in the Bhakti movement is also an example. The Krishna we learn about in the Bhagavad Gita (discussed in the sacred texts section, page 107) is not the same as the Krishna popularly worshiped. The life of Krishna Gopala, the "cowherd Krishna," was told in the Bhagavata Purana approximately at the start of the ninth century C.E.

This Purana put in writing a legend that had been growing for centuries. Krishna Gopala is portrayed as an enchanting youth who, while playing his flute in the forests, attracted the love of all the local women. They came to be known as the Gopis. Radha is the main Gopi, and Krishna's lover. By loving him, the Gopis came to know ultimate spiritual reality. This is the Krishna that the Hare Krishna movement is based on, and the love of this Krishna is widespread through the Bhakti movement.

Meditate on filling yourself with Divine love, and after tapping into that Divine taproot, interact with others throughout the day from your Awakened Heart. Make your choices in life from this same center of love. Protect it by making choices that support you living from your heart. Trust that all born out of this Awakened Heart is in your highest and best interest, and your best way of serving God.

To put Bhakti Yoga into practice in everyday life is to come from the heart. Awaken your heart to love as Divine Service.

I recall one application of Bhakti in everyday life. When I was a young man, I did our family's grocery shopping once a week. At the store where I shopped I became aware of one of the checkout clerks who worked there. There was something about him. He interacted with everybody playfully and brought a smile to everyone's face, just by checking out their groceries and engaging people in the most heartful way. It got so I would look forward to shopping day and my chance to watch him in action. I always stood in his line, even if it was the longest. One day I got up the courage to ask him how he was always able to be so happy. I'll never forget his answer. "Happiness and joy . . . why, I figure these are the only two things I have that no one can ever tax or take away!" He knew.

The Path of Karma Yoga

Here karma refers to work and action, any action, including thoughts. As mentioned previously, *yoga* means "union." The path of Karma Yoga is uniting all of one's actions with God. Workers and "householders," whose lives prevent constant devotional worship, specifically favor this path. Duty calls, the children need to be fed, or it's time to go to work. Karma Yoga is accepting your station in life and fulfilling your duties with dignity and honor, and dedicating the fruits of your activities to God. It's planting the seeds with no thought of the harvest. It's doing what you do because that is what you are called to do, with no thought of the outcome. It's fulfilling your responsibilities as spiritual service. Ideally, Karma Yoga would include the principles of right livelihood by finding employment in ways that help in the world and create no harm. It is the path of finding the Supreme Truth through work.

Karma Yoga: *The path of dedicating all of one's work in the world to the service of God.*

Many of us are enticed by the spiritual path, but we have families, jobs, bills, and other responsibilities. Following the path of Karma Yoga, we can accept our true station in life, and fulfill our responsibilities as opportunities for spiritual service. This is considered a most direct way of purifying one's personal karma accumulated in this life. It is also taught that practicing Karma Yoga softens the severity of past-life karma—if it is in one's karma to receive a knife wound in this life, by practicing Karma Yoga, this could be reduced to a mere pinprick.

The Bhagavad Gita, one of the most sacred of Hindu scriptures, teaches that the path of Karma Yoga extends even into mental activities. The Buddha taught that mind is a forerunner of all things; as you *think*, so you shall *become*. The Gita is a bit more pointed when it says that a person, who controls his actions, but not his mind, is a hypocrite—strong medicine and a powerful lesson. We can imagine someone sitting as in meditation, but actually lost in the fantasy of the worldly life of desires, fears, hopes, and plans. Or, in a more mundane sense, imagine someone who meets you and smiles and shakes your hand, but is thinking cutting, unfriendly thoughts about you. This is definitely not the way. The path of selfless conduct within right activity is encouraged, offering every act and its rewards to God.

The material going on inside our own head seems so private, like we shouldn't be held accountable for it. Picture your thoughts as your karma-makers, for good or for ill. If you can gain control of your mind by staying in the observer mode, not entering into judgments, and picturing this as spiritual service, you are practicing Karma Yoga at the subtle level.

The Vedanta Path: Jnana Yoga and the Path of Knowledge

Vedanta, meaning "end of the Vedas," holds particular allegiance to the Upanaishads (explored in sacred texts section, see page 107), and is called the "path of knowledge." This is Jnana Yoga, union through knowledge. Those who follow Vedanta are not interested in cosmology, or how creation came into manifestation. They start with the premise "Only Brahman is real, and all else is illusionary." Their understanding that Ultimate Reality could not possibly change, come into form as a personal God and leave, supports this—Ultimate Reality would be immutable, eternal, and unchanging. Ultimate Reality is said to exist on a separate order of being from anything our mind or senses could put before us.

The Vedanta path places no stock in petitioning the gods for their assistance; enlightenment will come through one's own effort of renouncing the phenomenal world. Vedanta teaches that the entire manifest world, including personal gods, is illusionary with the only reality being Brahman-Atman. The question "What is the source of self?" is the only question worth pursuing. We can imagine this as the "witness point" of consciousness, turning inward on itself and gazing toward the source, rather than anything in the manifest realm. To the manifest world, Vedanta offers its famous response: *neti, neti, neti,* meaning, "not this, not this, not this."

A Neti, Neti, Neti Meditation

Neti, neti, neti, is a very effective form of meditation on the question, "What is the source of the self?" Whatever you can think of, the answer has to be *neti, neti, neti,* "not this, not this, not this."

Sit in meditation with the object of your meditation being, "What is the source of self?" Take inventory of the ways you experience life and ask if any of these are the true source of self. Ask yourself, "Am I my thoughts?" The answer would have to be no, *neti*. If you can observe your thoughts, who is doing the observing? To the question "Am I my body?" again the answer would be neti; if you can observe your body, this could not be the source of self. "Am I my emotions?" "Am I my senses?" Neti, neti. With each question, drop deeper into the observer, the witness point of consciousness. Imagine turning the witness inward upon itself, no longer looking into your individual life, now gazing inward to the eternal Atman.

Although there are many branches within Vedanta, the Advaita, or nondual philosophy, as put forward by the great Shankara in his commentary on the Brahma Sutra during the eighth century C.E., is the dominant influence. Shankara is widely regarded as one of the world's great philosophers, and although many others have contributed to the greater understanding of Vedanta, Shankara's contributions reign supreme.

Three levels of ordinary consciousness are identified: (1) the purely subjective and fanciful world of dreams and daydreams; (2) the seemingly stable world of objective reality; and (3) the realm of the gods. Ultimate Reality is seen as beyond all of these, and is said to exist on another order of being.

Maya, Goddess of Illusion

In referring to the separate orders of reality, Vedanta teaches that there is no direct logical link between them. In between realms is *Maya,* goddess of illusion. The phenomenal world is the working of Maya, thus illusionary. Maya is what we encounter when we reach the outer limits of what the mind can comprehend. When the ego realm tries to peer into the realm of Brahman, it looks through Maya, and is not to be trusted. Shankara taught this to be "superimposition." All troubles begin when the ego-encapsulated self identifies with that which is truly

Maya: ***Goddess of illusion. Maya veils ultimate truth with what appears as reality.***

Atman, and that which is Atman identifies with that which is of the separate self.

For example, look at the statement "I have a headache." The "I" that Shankara encourages us to identify with is Atman, beyond form, and thus, not able to have a headache. Shankara would prefer it said, "I am in a body that is having a headache." While studying this, I found a direct application. I have been periodically plagued by headaches, particularly when I push too hard. One morning while studying Shankara's writings, I was distracted by an ensuing headache. Shankara's material inspired me to go into meditation to align with that part of me that *wasn't* having a headache. I could feel the headache and focused my attention on specifically where I felt the pain in my body. I kept settling further back into the place within me that was doing the observing, and—lo and behold—this part of me was not having a headache! Ah.

Vedanta distinguishes between the True Self and the apparent self—Atman and *jiva*. Jiva is the individual soul within Atman. It is the jiva that reincarnates, life after life, carrying the lessons and challenges from previous incarnations. Strong emotional experiences form impressions upon the subtle energy field of the jiva. These are stored within the psyche as *vasanas*, psychological leanings and desires that pull one toward certain life experiences. This is the understanding of how karma works and follows us life after life.

Vasanas: *Psychological leanings and desires that pull one toward certain life experiences.*

What does this mean to the Western seeker? First, it sheds light on the process of reincarnation. There is continuity from one life to the next. One teacher was asked by a student, "Exactly what is it that reincarnates?" The teacher responded, "Mostly your bad habits." This gets to the point; we are creating our future reality by the choices we make in this life. It is in this life that we have the capacity to make choices. The high road and the low road present themselves each day. The choices you make, even in terms of how you react to life itself, are what is registered in the jiva and continue after life, to be reborn in the next perfect incarnation for your energy field.

The teachings reveal that even if you do not achieve enlightenment in this life, but you make honorable attempts to awaken, this effort will promise a favorable rebirth that will support your further awakening. Again, there's continuity.

Applying this principle retrospectively leads to the awareness that your current life is an accumulation of the lessons learned, and not learned, from previous lives. Eternity is a long time. It stretches backward and forward. When we grasp this, it gives us encouragement for getting it together now. The wheel goes around and around, the sense of "I" continues in a neverending panorama of choices made.

The seed of Atman is within each jiva and it is taught that all beings will eventually attain liberation. The method of attaining liberation is by purifying the self of all desires. The physical self and the ego are not seen as real, thus renouncing attachments to their callings is a primary focus. In its most dramatic expression, we see the path of the ascetic renouncing all worldly attachments, a revered tradition in India.

Short of literally renouncing the world and heading off to a life in an ashram, the principle of renunciation and taking refuge in Atman is a worthy practice. While going through a particularly human drama such as jealousy, grudge, anger, or the numberless others, try renouncing the jiva, your personal involvement with the situation and realize that Maya is around. Know that through the jiva it seems very real, yet you refuse to identify with the experience. Identify with the Atman in you, the place that has never been wounded or soiled by the jiva's experiences. You are going through the experience, and, simultaneously, you are not.

Try the attitude of "So this is what humans go through," as a method for pulling out of the jiva's grip. In the middle of an intense drama, like jealously or worrying about your children or a relationship, practice this method of getting to that vantage point of "So this is what humans go through." You detach from the experience by realizing it is not just *you* going through this, it's a *human* scenario and humans all over the world are going through this particular challenge. It's a human lesson, not just yours. By not identifying with the apparent truth of the situation, it helps you to pull out of the illusion. From this detached view, you not only see creative alternatives to the real-life situation in front of you, you also help restore peace in the situation by being in a deep place of peace yourself, seeing the situation and seeing beyond it, simultaneously.

I have seen this principle in action within my family. We have raised four sons and experienced all the joys, sorrows, and dramas this entails. Although my meditation practice has been with me most of my adult life, there have been gaps, periods of time, when I wasn't meditating regularly. I noticed a correlation over the years between these gaps and family traumas. Invariably, times of trouble in the family were times that I was not meditating. It became clear to me that there was no center in the family, no calm spot, no deep peace.

I learned that one of the ways I could be most helpful for the family was to return to meditation practice. It always helped. Of course, the responsibility of being "father" dictated that I play a certain role in the situation; but in meditation, I could see this as a role. We are all learning life lessons; I am learning lessons about being a father, my son is learning lessons of being a young man, and behind it all is the eternal peace of Atman. You see it as a play being acted out and know that "this, too, shall pass."

Vedanta does allow for a personal God, Ishvara, but somewhat begrudgingly, preferring to believe in only Brahman. Ishvara is seen as the vehicle through which Brahman becomes manifest. Ramakrishna explains how there can be a personal God if one believes only in Brahman. He uses the analogy of water. In its natural state it is formless, but at the poles, where it is very cold, it freezes into a solid form. In the same way Brahman is the formless ocean and Ishvara is the personal God, frozen into apparent form so that we humans can conceptualize that which is beyond our capacity to understand. Without water, there can be no ice, without Brahman, there can be no personal God.

Ishvara is seen as born out of an interaction between Brahman and Maya. So, although accepted as a form of worship, still, it is not considered the highest path.

"*Tat tvam asi,*" one of the most familiar sayings from Hinduism, epitomizes the high road. It translates as "That thou art," where *that* refers to Atman. When one awakens to the True Self, Atman, the same for you as for me, or anyone, then one sees self in all things. Enlightenment—moksha—occurs by identifying with the eternal self that stands behind all manifestation. "Tat tvam asi." Vedanta teaches that this knowledge brings moksha and release from the wheel of death and rebirth.

Vedanta also teaches a path of purification by following certain precepts: disciplining the senses, practicing loving-kindness, surrendering to the guru, harmlessness, gentle considerate speech, meditation of texts, and affirming identity with Brahman through visualization and pranayama. These practices are seen as purifying the jiva so one can merge with Atman/Brahman. Although it's called the path of knowledge, its aim is beyond what the mind can grasp.

Here we find a key distinction between Western and Hindu thought. Western thought relies on the senses to verify reality; Hindu thought specifically rejects this, and says that consciousness exists on a separate order of being. What in the West we describe as consciousness, Vedanta asserts as still in the realm of the mind, and thus not true consciousness, which lies beyond, in a separate order of being from what the mind can understand.

In *Hinduism,* Steven Cross writes, "Enlightenment is the correction of an error, a change in self-identity. It occurs at the moment when we no longer identify with the limited individual self (which continues to appear but has ceased to be important to us) but with the unchanging beam of consciousness which stands behind and illumines all experience."[3]

The life story of Ramana Maharshi perhaps most clearly illuminates the teachings of Advaita Vedanta.[4] As a teenager, he experienced a spontaneous vision of his own death—the ceremony and cremation. As he watched, he had the sudden illumination of knowing that if he could witness even his death, and yet maintain consciousness, he obviously was not his body. From that moment on, he spent his entire life inquiring as to the source of Self. He taught that to continually meditate on the question "What is the source of self?" is all that is necessary to awaken.

The Sankhya School and the Philosophy of Hinduism

Although Hinduism is more of an aggregate of many schools of thought, the Sankhya school has provided much of the philosophical underpinnings that support all of Hinduism. Much of the vocabulary of Hinduism has been adopted from the Sankhya, as they were the great namers. They named and identified the specific realms of consciousness and put forth a worldview that has been incorporated into many Hindu beliefs.

This mapping-out was not to substantiate existence, but to show the way out. They organized the world into categories, levels, and stages. This naming of the world was important—to *know* it was to be able to *transcend* it. The ultimate goal was not to know the world as a scientist, but rather as a mystic; understanding the nature of reality could liberate one from its constraints.

Sankhya identifying and naming is its great contribution to Hinduism, but it obviously presents a great deal of jargon. Bear with it. If you are to do any further reading on Hinduism and Eastern mysticism, you will frequently come across the vocabulary. Plus, the Sankhya philosophy puts forward a theory of creation that is profound in its own light, but also sheds light on the mechanics of karma, and how events manifest in life.

Purusha and Prakriti

The unfolding of creation begins with the dance of Purusha and Prakriti. These principles could be described as spirit *(Purusha)* and matter *(Prakriti)*. Much like the familiar yin and yang of Eastern teachings, Purusha and Prakriti are the two archetypal expressions behind all manifestation. It is through their interaction that all manifestation arises. Prakriti is the ground, the vehicle of manifestation for Purusha, the animating spark of spirit that brings life to that which was inert. Prakriti is pure potency, but without the animating spirit of Purusha, remains merely dormant potential.

The cosmic idea, called *Mahat,* or "word of God," sets Purusha and Prakriti into interaction. This causes a vibration in the *gunas,* a further subdivision of Prakriti. The *gunas* are the three energy strands that make up all of existence. They are: *rajas*, the principle of action; *sattva*, the principle of harmony; and *tamas*, the principle of inertia. Picture the image of Prakriti and Purusha interacting in such a way that creates a vibration; much like a harp playing endless variations of combinations and intensities of the three strings named rajas, sattva, and tamas.

Gunas: *The gunas are three energy strands that make up all existence: action, harmony, and inertia.*

This part of the story exists beyond the human realm—it is not happening because of humans or to humans—it is just happening. Enter human consciousness into the story. The highest mental faculty of the human potential is *buddhi*. This is the intuitive mind that can perceive these subtle currents of the gunas. However, the buddhi is also sensitive to the needs of the ego, called the *ahamkara*, or I-maker. The ahamkara gets most of its information from the manas, the rational mind and the senses.

We can see from the diagram at right that everything tends downward, away from the spiritual. The trick is to reverse the process. Instead of letting the ego (ahamkara) dictate to the higher mind (buddhi) the right choice of action, you make the ahamkara become allegiant to buddhi by denying the information coming to you through *manas* and the world of the senses.

To complicate the issue—and add more jargon—is the workings of karma. When you have emotional reactions to events in your life, this creates impressions on your energy field. These impressions are called samskaras. Many samskaras in the same area of life create a huge impression on your energy field called vasanas. These vasanas are subconscious motivations that drive you to certain types of behavior. Your reaction to the behavior creates new samskaras and sets the gunas vibrating in yet another unique way, which continue to manifest neverending combinations of reality—thus it goes on and on. This describes the workings of karma, which reveals itself to be nothing other than the energetic total of our choices.

Although the philosophy of Hinduism can seem daunting, it can be simplified. A Sikh friend and teacher of mine, Arjun Singh

Sumthershe, put it together in a delightful story. We were at a dinner party and when asked about the Sikh path, he began his story. First he produced a small, hand-pinched clay pot. He said the clay pot is like the body. He next poured olive oil into the pot and said this is like our mental body, manas. He then pinched off some rolled cotton and rubbing it within his palms with olive oil produced a wick. Submerging the wick in the pot with just the tip exposed, he told this was like our intellect, buddhi, the higher faculty of the mind that can perceive intuitive truth.

He then took a box of stick matches and, lighting a match, he told us the flame represented the teachings. He kept lighting matches and holding them away from the wick until they burned out and told us that all the teachings in the world might be present, but if we don't touch them with our intuitive mind, the flame of truth will not light our intellect. He finally touched a burning match to the wick and it ignited with its own flame. The teaching was evident; when we go into the teachings and

Mahat ("In the beginning was the word...")

↓ ***Purusha*** and ***Prakriti*** . . .

↓ The ***gunas*** set into vibration . . .

↓ The ***Buddhi*** receives these subtle vibrations . . .

↓ The ***Ahamkara*** interprets this as personal . . .

↓ The ***manas*** gather supporting evidence to make this a personal issue.

seek the flame of eternal truth, this ignites our own inner flame of truth.

His teachings went on. He directed our attention to the flame and said that although we could see the effect of the flame in the light it produced, we couldn't see the light itself; it permeated everything. This invisible essence, he said, is God.

Although Arjun indulged my endless questions about the teachings, paths, and techniques of Hinduism and Sikhism, he was at a point on his path where the teachings held no interest for him, preferring to stay immersed in the Divine presence by constantly being aware of Divine grace. He knew the teachings, but they no longer held value for him. If you are in Chicago, you don't have to look for a bus to Chicago.

I found it interesting that most of the people at the dinner party affirmed that the teachings were not necessary, were merely intellectual banter, and the true path is surely staying anchored in God Realization at all times. If one is truly at a point of development that passions, desires, negative thinking patterns, and anger no longer disturb the God-centered consciousness, then indeed, this is the high path. But if a person has not achieved a tranquil mind, then the teachings are there to help break the patterns of negativity and self-destructiveness.

When a student asked if the practices and meditations were necessary, Sri Ramakrishna explained it this way, "When upon hearing the name of God in all of his manifestations, you immediately are overwhelmed by Divine bliss, then you can let go of the chants, austerities, practices, and so forth. Until then the techniques are necessary to break old patterns and prepare the mind to receive direct illumination."[5]

Hidden in this philosophy is a key to freedom. You can use this as a map for liberating yourself from an event-based view of life, to see the energy behind it, and beyond. First off, the map provides an understanding of how events manifest in your life.

The gunas are the energy behind the events manifesting before our eyes. However, our eyes are looking through Maya, illusion. Maya creates a very believable screen that the ego is going to try to make personal—and will—if you let it. The trick is to see this happening and to know that it is illusion, Maya at work, like the projected image in Plato's cave. But how to get out of the cave when it all looks so convincingly real, right before your eyes in the event world?

The first step is to see the big picture, to know what is going on from your buddhi perspective, the witness. Learn to see the energy behind the event. The events are always made up of various degrees of the gunas, action, harmony, and inertia. This is an energy view of life—shift your attention away from the events and to the energy of the moment.

Rajas energy is hot, intense, passionate, fiery, and active. Sattva energy is harmonious, peaceful, at ease with the situation at hand. Tamas energy is slovenly, indulgent, weak, fearful, and resistant. Everything and every situation is a different combination of these three energy strands. This also applies to your natural temperament, your natural energy makeup that you return to, all things being equal. And, of course, various situations interact with your natural way of being and momentarily set the gunas to vibrate in a vibration consistent with your response.

If you do not compensate for the gunas, you will be locked into a perception from the ego, the I-maker, which justifies your current reaction. This is Plato's cave and the screen you are watching is made up of the events of your life, and it all seems so real. The screen justifies your current interpretation of reality, "Well, of course I'm mad, look at what just happened!" "Well, of course I'm angry, look what this person did!" "Well, of course I'm sad, and this is why . . ." This locks you into a view of reality that is always in response to the events of your life.

Look at the current event as a screen that you are projecting your energy on. Tell yourself that if it were not this current situation that was making you mad (angry, upset, frustrated, etc.) it would be a hundred others. Let go of the event as the important issue and work with the energy of the moment itself. Instead of being mad at . . ., just be mad. Instead of being frustrated because . . ., just be frustrated. Own the energy. If you do not own it, you cannot do anything with it, other than just reacting to whatever you think caused your experience.

If you own the energy, you can work with it. Energy is just energy. It can be transformed to other forms of energy by inner work, but first you have to own it. If you are locked into the label, the justifiable reason for feeling the way you do, you've given away your power to the situation you are reacting to. The energy builds and fires off at the target of your frustration, thus you end up giving your life force to the very issue you think you are against!

To let go of the label, the reason, gives you the freedom to work with the energy within yourself. Without the labels, it is merely the *energy* behind the way that you are feeling, not because of anything, just the way that you are with your energy. This works particularly well with issues of power like anger, frustration, irritation, and the like. Ask yourself: "What does the energy of the moment *feel* like?" "Where does the energy seem to resonate in my body, and how does it feel?" "What music are the gunas playing at this moment?"

I have an exercise in which I picture the frustrated, angry energy I'm feeling as a seething, dark ball low in my spine. Next, I let go of that image and focus on my heart and picture it as a fiery orb of energy. I breathe a couple of deep breaths into my heart and picture the flames dancing brightly. Then I go back to the image of the dark ball deep in my spine and breathe deep into it. On the in-breath I coax the dark ball up my spine and when it reaches my heart I picture all of the darkness and negativity being burned away, leaving clear, radiant energy. Now I'm free to express the energy any way I choose. I can work in my yard, I can work on a book, I can workout, or I can play. The energy has been transmuted.

Shake your Buddhi!

It can be seen that it is buddhi that stands between the true Self and the ego self. Buddhi perceives the higher truth of Atman, but is dissuaded by the ahamkara and its emotions. It is also subject to Maya and the illusions caused by the ahamkara taking personally something that was not. So, shake your buddhi! Demand that it awaken to its higher potential, and shake off the illusions of the separate self.

Moksha in the Sankhya Philosophy

The Sankhya philosophy does not support the notion of a personal God. It is not assistance from any deity that will bring liberation; it is personal effort and knowledge that can free the soul from endless cycles of death and rebirth. I once heard a saying, "The measure of greatness of a person's soul is in how unruffled he remains in the face of shocking news." This saying captures the Sankhya philosophy of liberation. The ahamkara, of course reacts to everything, so one learns not to identify with its reactions.

This is similar to the Dhozchen path of Buddhism, which teaches if one can learn to *not* react to situations, karma will not be created. Of course, this is not simply repressing the reactions; it is residing in the place in you that does not react.

Imagine being in a sudden, upsetting situation, such as getting fired, in an argument, or something equally upsetting. It happens. Moksha would come from residing in that place in you that is observing these things happening to you; not in reaction to it, but simply observing it. You stay mindful of yourself watching the experience even as you are going through the intensity of the moment. Even everyday annoyances, like traffic and other people's bad days, are opportunities for practicing this exercise of freedom—freedom from reaction.

Cycles of Time

The Hindu view of time stretches the imagination. First off, time is circular, not linear, in neverending cycles upon cycles. Four great ages, called *yugas,* are defined in a cycle from Golden Ages to Dark Ages and back again. This cycle of time is yet part of a larger cycle, a *mahayuga* of 4,320,000 years, which is yet part of a still-larger cycle, a *kalpa.* This leads to cycles of time millions of years in duration! Obviously, their view of time is vast.

There is a popular story in Hinduism. When a student asked, "How long have I been doing this reincarnational cycle?" the teacher replied, "Imagine a granite mountain one mile high, one mile wide, and one mile long. Imagine a bird with a silk scarf flies over the mountain once every 100 years and drags the scarf across the mountain. As long as it would take that bird to wear down the mountain with the scarf, that's how long you've been doing this."

It is understood that even creation itself will one day cease to exist in its manifest form, dissolving back into Brahman for a cycle of dormancy, to reemerge in another cycle of expression. I get the image of a huge cosmic whale with its eye open to creation and as the whale blinks, creation ceases, to reemerge on the next opening of the cosmic eye.

The Kali Yuga

In the Hindu calendar of time, we are now in the Kali Yuga. This is considered the Dark Age. Most accounts place it as beginning approximately 3,102 B.C.E. During the Kali Yuga, human mental faculties are their dullest and it is said that all of humanity will tend to stray away from the sacred, forget their prayers and practices, forgetting even to bless their food, and generally be lead by the desire for sensory gratification and grasping for material gain.

There is an interesting teaching considering merit during the Kali Yuga. It is thought that even a small conscious act of loving kindness in a Dark Age is worth the merit of a considerable spiritual act in another age. Even a little bit of spiritual integrity is said to gain considerable spiritual merit.

Even a small conscious act of loving-kindness in the Kali Yuga is worth the merit of a considerable spiritual act in another age.

This implies the degree of difficulty is accounted for in the larger scheme of things and even if you are only able to incorporate a small amount of spiritual growth in this life, due to the odds being against you, this would improve your future births to the same degree that would require considerable spiritual growth in a more spiritual age.

When I think of this teaching, it helps me to better understand what looks like sure madness in the modern world, and makes it seem like more of a miracle that any teachings get to us at all in the Kali age. Thank God for the teachings! It is grace to have spiritual teachings available when nothing else makes sense. Being a spiritually minded individual in a Dark Age can feel lonely; there's not much support, and so much of what you see in the world is in direct contrast to a spiritual life. When you look out into the modern world and wonder if we've gone to hell in a handbasket, remember that we are in a Dark Age and this, too, shall pass. Be thankful for the precious teachings you do find.

At least one authority, Sri Yukteswar (Yogananda's guru) disputes the general belief that we are still in the Kali Yuga. In *The Holy Science,* he cites evidence that humanity moved out of the Dark Age in approximately 1599 C.E.[6] According to his credible calculations, we are on the ascending phase of the Dwapara Yuga. Although still dense compared to more enlightened yugas, during Dwapara Yuga humanity develops increased mental capacity to understand the physical world and feels the promptings to return to more spiritual practices. Humanity's mental capacity is not yet developed to the degree of understanding the workings of the intuitive mind and spiritual reality as it will be in future ages, but at least it is on the ascent.

Yogananda speaks of shortcutting the normal process of evolution in *Autobiography of a Yogi.* He teaches that the incarnating ego identity normally takes one million years to achieve liberation from Maya, but by practicing the techniques of Kriya Yoga, one can shortcut this to a matter of years, or within this lifetime.[7] Kriya involves a yogic technique for awakening to higher levels of consciousness. These techniques will be explored in the Raja Yoga section.

The Path of Raja Yoga

The yoga school of thought breaks from the Sankhya tradition in that it believes that knowledge alone is not sufficient to experience moksha. Action and training are viewed as essential for liberation. As we know, yoga means "union" or "yoke;" to practice yoga is to yoke oneself in union with the Divine. We are quite familiar with yoga in the West, with yoga centers cropping up all across the country. As an outsider to yoga, it looks like just body postures and flexibility. But those who take up the practice of yoga know that the postures are only one of the components of the yoga path.

Patanjali, in the third century C.E., set forth the teachings that are the basis of the yoga path. His four-volume set, *The Yoga Sutras,* is of such importance that, even to this day, other teachers of yoga will refer to it as the true source. It is understood that Patanjali did not create this system of knowledge, it had been practiced for thousands of years, but he was the first to record it in written form. Patanjali's work is both mystical and scientific. He maps out in specific detail the various stages of consciousness achieved through the practice of yoga. His system of yoga is called Ashtanga Yoga, and there are eight paths, or limbs.

The Eight Limbs of Ashtanga Yoga

The goal of the yoga system of Patanjali is to quiet the mind so that it may rest in complete absorption with the Divine. His philosophy is born out of the Sankhya understanding of the steps of creation, but differs in that knowledge is not seen as enough for liberation, the yogi must learn to quiet the restless mind through effort. There are eight steps to this path that begins with purifying one's lifestyle, then mastering certain postures and breathing techniques, and finally entering into meditation training.

Yama: Yama is the first step of the Eightfold Path of yoga. This is developing self-control by following five main precepts. *Ahimsa,* living with the intention of not causing harm or injury to anyone or anything, encapsulates all of the remaining precepts of being truthful, not stealing, expressing honorable sexuality, and not being covetousness (not grasping or wanting). This self-control is just as important in thought as in action. Ahimsa explains the mysterious "sacred cow" of Hinduism. The cow is sacred because all life is sacred and why Hindus are primarily vegetarians. The gentle cow is also the symbol of the sustaining aspect of life—giving more than it takes.

Niyama: Niyama describes the ethical practices one needs to develop. These include purification of the body and mind, practicing simplicity in all ways, cultivating contentment with one's life, and studying sacred texts to anchor the mind in God.

Asanas: These are the body postures we associate with yoga. They have been developed over the centuries and handed down through the generations. These postures have been specifically designed to help awaken the flow of life force throughout one's total energy field. Hatha Yoga takes these body postures as the core of the practice. Patanjali only says that the posture should be comfortable so one can stay in it a length of time, and that the back, neck and head should be in alignment.

Pranayama: Controlling and using the breath to awaken the movement of prana, the universal life force. Breath is the vehicle for visualizing the movement of energy, but it is the control and movement of prana—life force—that is the discipline. A pranayama meditation exercise is offered later in this chapter (see page 88).

Pratyahara: Consciously pulling your attention away from the sensory world. Withdrawing into the "yogic cave," the place within that prepares you for inward searching. Coming home.

Dharana: Concentration. The ability for holding your attention on the object of meditation, be it the tip of your nose, your third eye, your breath, or a particular concept.

Dhyana: Meditation. When you have succeeded at holding your attention with Dharana for an extended period of time, a sense of spaciousness begins to be experienced. Your sense of self-awareness disappears as a separate identity, replaced by a sense of oneness with all of life. You begin to receive input from whatever you are meditating upon.

Samadhi: Absorption. With Samadhi, the separate sense of self dissolves and is absorbed into the oneness. There is no separate person meditating, only oneness.

It is further taught that there are various degrees of Samadhi. Karma has its impact even at this level of experience. If one is aware of enjoying the Samadhi experience, even this dropping into the separate self, just by being aware of the delight, limits the experience. Even the subtlest waves of personal emotion are an action and have an effect, albeit a pleasant effect—this is definitely karma at its best! However, this tends to be self-perpetuating and attachments can form.

Seedless Samadhi: Beyond even Samadhi is seedless Samadhi. Even the gentlest waves of personal response are quieted, so that absolute union with the Divine occurs.

Patanjali's greatest contribution to the understanding of yoga is in his discriminating ability to describe the slightest nuances of the various stages of meditation. He states in the second sutra in Book I of the *Yoga Sutras,* "Yoga is control of the thought waves in the mind."[8] This sutra clearly states the intent of yoga: the practice of withdrawing the senses from all material and worldly issues to ultimately quiet the restless mind. This sutra teaches that physical yoga is only a setup for the deeper practice of yoga—quieting the mind and resting in God Realization.

The sutras illuminate the subtlest issues of how consciousness is disturbed by mind-waves, from the densest realms of lust and anger, to the most refined that influence the quality of Samadhi. It is interesting that in the entire Book I of the *Yoga Sutras,* not even once is a physical posture mentioned. In this tradition, the yogi is in training for quieting the mind-waves at all levels. Patanjali goes on to teach that when one has developed mastery of the mind, concentration can be held on anything from the most minute to the most expansive. When the mind-waves are quieted, one can enter into absorption with the object of meditation and come to know it directly.

Patanjali does allow for other techniques for experiencing the Divine. In Sutra 23, he proclaims that Samadhi can be reached quickly through devotion (bhakti), by intense concentration on Ishvara (God), and practicing japa (silent repetition of God's name).

The teachings go on to suggest that by identifying with *Ishvara,* one becomes spotless. Ishvara is the place within you that has never been soiled or affected by life. One becomes liberated from past karma and is altogether liberated in this state. Further techniques for achieving this are, performing japa with "OM," cultivating feelings of love and compassion, and experiencing suprasensitivity of the senses by focusing on the luminous state within.

Hatha Yoga

This is the form of yoga we are most familiar with in the West. The intent is to make the body a suitable instrument for experiencing the Divine. The postures and asanas that have been handed down through the ages are designed to open the subtle energy channels within the body. Working with both breath (pranayama) and postures (asanas), the practitioner experiences increased health and vitality. There are an abundance of quality Hatha Yoga teachers, books, and videos available, so I will defer to other sources for the teachings about postures, techniques, etc.

Starting a Yoga Practice

There are many types of yoga practices to choose from. Some schools teach relaxation, some focus on strength and agility, and others are more aerobic; one is not necessarily better than the other. Find the type of practice that fits your particular needs.

Entering into a yoga practice is a proactive method for doing deep work on yourself. Westerners have grown up in an allopathic culture, which means you do work on the self when there is a problem and you need to overcome it. This leads to a therapy culture for those who are hungry to do deep personal work. If the need is there to do deep work on yourself, yoga is a method for engaging this discipline proactively—not to overcome a problem, but to do the deep work for its own rewards.

First, find a qualified teacher. It is not that yoga is dangerous without a teacher; it is more about the tremendous benefit that comes from having qualified feedback. The subtle adjustments a teacher can make in your postures make all the difference in the world. When we read of Patanjali's view of yoga, we realize that the postures are part of a larger practice. The postures set up a meditational practice by liberating energy that was previously blocked, allowing it to flow freely through the entire system. More than a foundation, the postures themselves help to awaken the chakras (the energy centers within the body to be discussed later). Concentration (Dharana) can greatly facilitate this awakening.

We'd like to think that we could enter into the meditative state with each posture, but this is not typical. However, concentration can be employed with great benefit. Some of the postures require strength, and at first, it might not be there, but with practice it comes. Concentration is vital—you can't chat and do yoga. You can chat or watch television and stretch, but yoga is maximized by concentration. Specifically, what is going on within the body with each posture? Focus your attention on the specific sensations arising in your body. Use your attention to help steady your posture. Steady your breath; find your center.

If you choose to deepen a posture, do so on the out-breath, and then, ever so gently, ease off the deepened stretch on the in-breath. With practice, the body strengthens. You become steady in the posture, and your concentration can shift away from your muscles and tendons, and toward the subtle energy currents just beneath the surface. Feel this prana move through you with each posture, concentrate on how the energy is moving and feel the awakening of your subtle energy bodies. We will go through one posture as a means of illustration.

The Head-Knee Pose

The head-knee pose shown works well, and, ideally, would be done for both the left and right sides, although we will only discuss one way here. First sit on the floor with your legs straight out in front of you. Start with your hands on your thighs and concentrate on your spine. Straighten it from the tailbone, through the neck, and right up through the head. Concentrate on lengthening your spine; pull your spine up and out of your pelvis and extend your torso and head. Use a mirror if necessary to see if your head is centered over your shoulders or slouched forward.

Now pull your left foot and place it on the inside of your thigh on the extended right leg. Place it as high up your

Figure 3. KNEE-TO-TOE EXERCISE (FIRST POSITION).

thigh as you can toward your groin. Extend your left knee out to the left with your bent leg on, or toward, the floor. Now reach both hands straight overhead and again imagine lengthening your spine. Next, fold forward, bending at the waist, remembering to keep the spine straight. Reach your hands toward your feet and clasp them if you can, or grab your ankles, or shins if that is what you can do. Keep your spine straight, as if there were a broomstick from your tailbone right up through your head, and continue to fold forward on the out-breath.

Figure 4. KNEE-TO-TOE (SECOND POSITION).

On the in-breath, follow your attention to where you feel the tightness and burning. On the out-breath, breathe into that place where you feel tension, most likely your hamstrings on the back side of your outstretched leg, and imagine melting it with your attention and deepen your stretch ever so slightly.

On the in-breath, just be with the posture and the sensations. Picture yourself breathing in prana, and on the out-breath, picture the prana moving through energy channels in the body that are being opened by the posture (see illustration on page 106 for energy channels). When you are ready to pull up out of the posture, again sit upright and extend both legs in front of you. Now stop and simply feel the posture's effects. Repeat on the other side of your body by pulling your right foot up to the inside of your left thigh.

Individual differences in the posture are huge; some people are able to lay their bodies flat on their legs and others are barely able to fold forward at all. This is the beauty of yoga. Everybody is

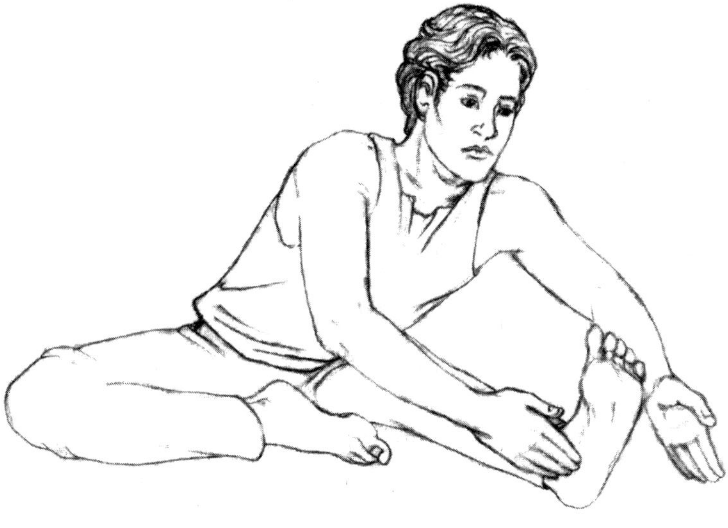

Figure 5. KNEE-TO-TOE (FINISHING POSITION).

doing the same work on themselves—going to the point of tension in the body and breathing through it. There is no competition in yoga, everyone is there to do their own personal work, and it is the same work no matter where you are at in mastering the posture. Be patient with yourself. Be assured you will see significant improvement with practice. Yoga ages well—it is one physical activity that you can actually improve upon with age.

Meditation after a yoga series is particularly beneficial. The body is stretched and aligned and therefore doesn't demand attention. Plus, the subtle energy currents are awakened, creating optimum conditions for meditation.

Pranayama Yoga

Pranayama is the yoga science of using breath to awaken the flow of prana. Prana is the life force that animates all of life. With pranayama practices, you are focusing on your breath, but you are also visualizing prana moving through you with each breath.

A Pranayama exercise

Sit in a posture with your spine as straight as possible. Put your left hand in your lap, palm up. Raise your right hand to your face with your thumb just touching your right nostril and your ring finger just touching your left nostril. Let your index and middle fingers just touch your brow, and simply relax your little finger.

First take a few deep breaths through both nostrils until you feel centered. Now gently close your right nostril with pressure from your thumb and breathe in through your open left nostril. Hold your breath for a moment and then gently close the left nostril with pressure from the ring finger and simultaneously release the pressure from your thumb, opening the right nostril. Breathe out through the open right nostril. Next, keeping the right nostril open, breathe in, hold your breath for a moment, and alternate the open nostril and breathe out the left side. Repeat this cycle for several minutes.

As you center into the activity, add a visualization. While you breathe in on the left side, picture yourself filling your feminine, receptive side of your being with prana, or life force. As you hold your breath at the top of the breath, center your attention on your brow and visualize the masculine and feminine aspects of your being merging as one. When you breathe out the right side, visualize emptying the masculine aspect of your being of all that it has been holding

Figure 6. PRANAYAMA EXERCISE. *Inset:* SIDE VIEW.

(anger, carrying the load of responsibility, frustration, etc. Men or women, we all have this masculine energy.).

Now reverse the process. As you breathe in on the right side, picture yourself filling your masculine nature with prana. Feel your courage and strength growing. At the top of the in-breath, pull your attention to your brow and image the yin-yang energies coming together. As you breathe out the left side, imagine yourself emptying and letting go of all attachments from your feminine nature (relationship issues, worries and concerns about others, emotional issues, etc.).

Use the image of a mountain. On the in-breath through the open left nostril, you are ascending the mountain on the left side. As you hold your breath, you are at the peak. As you breathe out the right nostril, picture yourself descending on the right side of the mountain. Then back up, to the peak, and down the other side.

After several repetitions of this cycle you can drop your right hand to your lap and continue the activity without the aid of your thumb and finger. At this stage, it is your intent and visualization that guides the breath and prana. Even if some air gets in the nostril you are not intending to breathe through, your focused concentration on the same path of energy as before creates the desired effect.

Now complete your meditation by breathing through both nostrils simultaneously and visualize drawing prana up the sushumna (picture the sushumna as a hollow bamboo tube from your tailbone to the crown of your head). On the in-breath, pull the energy up your spine, fill with it as you hold your breath, and offer it as a blessing as you breathe out into the world. After a few deep, refreshing breaths, simply rest in your awakened energy field.

This exercise immediately balances your energy field and can be used, even in an abbreviated form, to immediately restore balance. It balances the left and right hemispheres of the brain and also the masculine/feminine polarity.

Mystics know that on the wings of breath you can breathe anything into the body: love, courage, compassion, joy, clarity, etc. A variation of the above exercise is to visualize breathing in one of these qualities on your in-breath, filling yourself with this quality as you hold your breath, and then offer this quality to the world as a blessing on the out-breath. The image of the dialogue balloon in the comics can be useful. Put whatever quality you want in the balloon and picture breathing this into yourself on the in-breath.

The Chakras

The chakras are one of the great jewels that have come to us from the Hindu teachings. They provide a precise map to the human energy system and the seven distinct levels of consciousness. This is the energy blueprint for the human operating system, and to know your chakras is know how you are meant to operate at optimum, and precisely which chakra is out of balance when your energy system is out of whack.

Chakra means "spinning wheel," and can be perceived as a vortex of energy. There are seven main chakras aligned in front of the spine from the tailbone to the crown of the head. They are not physical, but energetic, and each one governs a particular aspect of the human experience, from the instinctual to the refined.

Each person has all of the chakras and they can never be fully blocked—that is, if you are alive! To the degree that they function differently in decidedly different people, we all have all the chakras. They are your connection to the universal life force. They store and distribute the energy for all of your life activities. From the most physical of activities to the subtlest of meditations, the chakras have a direct role.

The chakras are not only centers of energy; they are the seven distinct levels of consciousness. Looking at life through each chakra is an entirely different experience. It is like different floors in a building—you get off at a given floor, you see something entirely different than if you get off on a different floor. The chakras are a map to all of the floors (levels of consciousness) available and studying them can help you see when you are stuck on a given floor, thinking this viewpoint is all of reality. The map shows the way out of conflict with life and points the way to live in harmony, in touch with your innate creativity and aligned with inner guidance.

Balance is the key to working with the chakras. When the energy is balanced at a particular chakra, it naturally rises to the next. It is not as if you have to push the energy to the upper chakras, it is naturally designed to happen, as long as there are

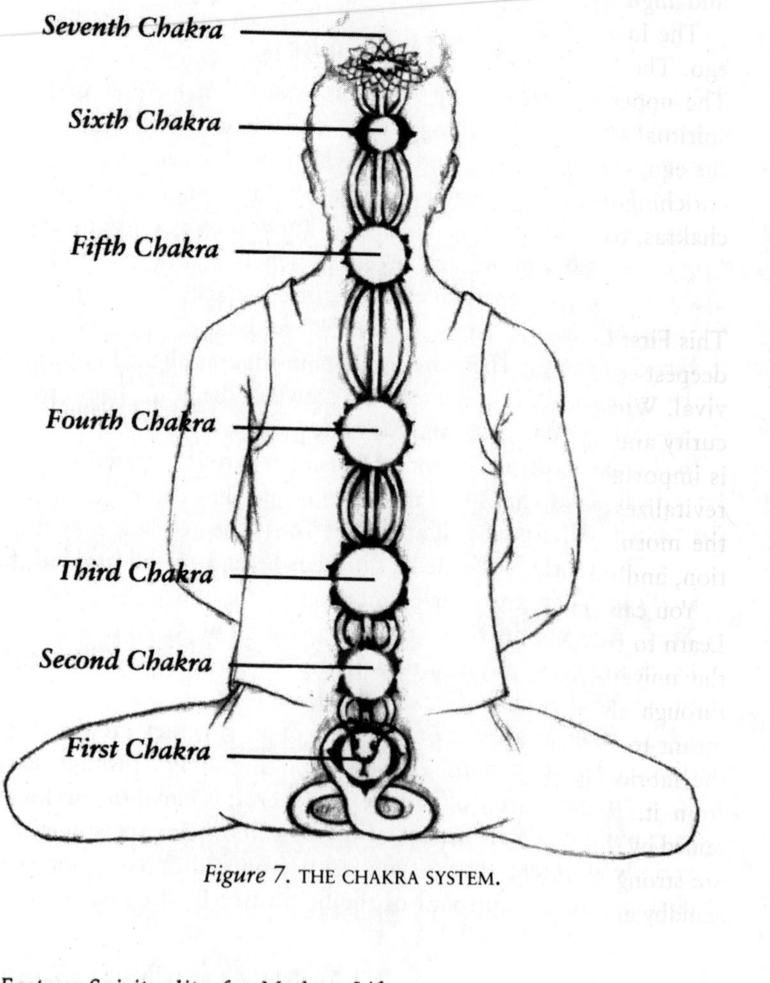

Figure 7. THE CHAKRA SYSTEM.

not imbalances in the lower chakras. Imbalances create events and justifiable issues that demand your attention at the imbalanced chakra. This constrains your attention, and consciousness is limited to the chakra demanding attention. As you bring the energy back into balance, it naturally rises on its own.

For suggestions on activities to balance each of the chakras, refer to my previous book *Chakras for Beginners*. The important consideration here is to realize there already is a point of balance within each chakra—you don't make it nor achieve it, you *find* it and *align* with it.

The lower three chakras are dominated by the needs of the ego. The Fourth Chakra awakens us to the needs of the soul. The upper chakras animate our connection to collective and spiritual levels of consciousness. This is the energetic dance of the ego, soul, and spirit, ideally all supporting, interacting, and enriching each other. Energy would freely move through all chakras, balanced within themselves and each other.

First Chakra

This First Chakra is also called the Root Chakra, and it is your deepest connection to your animal nature and instincts for survival. When balanced, you feel secure; when imbalanced, insecurity and fear are experienced. For a balanced First Chakra, it is important to have found your right place on the Earth that revitalizes your animal nature. If you walk out your door in the morning and the environment itself, the climate, vegetation, and the feel of the land revitalizes you, you are there.

You can't create security, you have to feel it and enter into it. Learn to trust that you are part of the universal life force expressed through all of nature and you are meant to be here. You are part of the fabric of nature, not separate from it. Know that you are sustained by the same prana that animates all of nature. Your instincts are strong with this balance, and fear is like a smoke alarm, on standby and ready to report danger, but not always sounding.

First Chakra: *Survival. Base of the spine. Fight or flight instincts. Your connection to the Earth. Security and fear issues.*

When the First Chakra is not balanced, you can feel insecure, ungrounded, and not in touch with your animal nature. The First Chakra is the densest and furthest away from spirit, thus, when unbalanced, your attention is pulled away from spirit and into the densest aspects of the material world. When unbalanced, a "survivor mentality" takes over. When surviving is on the line, morals, values, and ethics seem to get sidestepped. Everything feels threatening. Identifying yourself as a survivor also sets excessively low standards—surviving.

If you are locked in fear, find small ways to embrace life to ease out of the threatened place. Pet an animal, embrace a tree, or find counsel with a mountain stream. This helps break the First Chakra illusion of feeling absolutely separate and isolated from life.

Second Chakra

With an awakened Second Chakra, surviving is not enough and you want to enjoy your life and the sensory world. This is the chakra of pleasure and delight of the senses—sexuality and sensuality. The lure of pleasure can pull us to the most base, or become polished to appreciate the most refined. The ability to appreciate beauty, to enjoy the embrace of love, to taste the sweet taste of fruit or the luxury of chocolate; yes, life without an awakened Second Chakra would be bland and lacking joy. But the quest for pleasure can be neverending until one has truly learned to enter *into* the pleasure and not simply chase it. Without balance, attachments and even addictions can readily form from Second Chakra pleasures.

Second Chakra: ***Pleasure and Beauty. Just above the pubic ridge. Your capacity to enjoy the experience of life. The senses and the experience of pleasure. At the higher level, artistic sensitivity and appreciation for beauty.***

A balanced Second Chakra is the sweet kiss of life. You know how to enjoy life's simple pleasures and have learned how to express this enjoyment in many ways. You are not attached to any one source for enjoying life. With an awakened Second Chakra, you take the skill wherever you go, and voila! Life's enjoyable wherever you are. You have learned how to appreciate and enjoy sensory experiences without grasping for more. Instead of chasing pleasure, you experience it, by bringing gratification right to the core of your being. A balanced Second Chakra could be described by the saying, "To experience more joy in your life, spend more time wanting what you have and less time wanting what you don't have."

When the Second Chakra is not balanced, too much or too little focus on pleasure can result. The tantalizing sensory experiences can become quite addictive, and it is easy to get hooked on the chase for pleasure through sex, food, drugs, and alcohol. The opposite is just as troublesome. If the pleasure principle is repressed, bitterness results with feelings of being unloved and unappreciated. Men worry about their virility, women over their attractiveness. A lack of balance, either way, causes attention to be drawn to this arena to an excessive degree.

To restore balance, more attention must be brought to the appreciation of all experiences. In the middle of a hug, or enjoying a beautiful sunset, or listening to something beautiful and tasting something exquisite, stop for just half a moment and truly *feel* your appreciation of the moment. Without appreciation, you run right past life's great treasures, grasping for more. By cultivating your capacity to enjoy life's simple pleasures, you experience deeper satisfaction, and the illusion of needing more, or less, is broken.

Third Chakra

You awaken to issues concerning power with the Third Chakra. A balanced Third Chakra brings the effective use of will power. You know how to say "No" when you mean no, and "Yes" when you mean yes. You feel you have some control over your life with confidence that you can act on your plans and initiate activity when you choose to. You have learned to take charge of a situation if that is what is required, and how to back off when appropriate. Your power is not just in external issues, more importantly, you have developed self-control, and an effective life is the result.

When the Third Chakra is not balanced, issues concerning will power—either too much or too little—will surface. "Power corrupts," the old saying goes. The thrill of conquest and the rush of adrenaline from competitive energy can be addictive and the controlling, domineering, manipulative personality can result. Signals of this imbalance are the hair-trigger temperament at the extreme and, more commonly, the inability to surrender control in most situations with a need to be "right" in any argument. The opposite imbalance leads to a lack of will and feelings of being a victim of life, ineffectual, and uncertain. When this is the case, you feel like nothing in your life is of your choice, you are led around by circumstances and other people's expectations.

Third Chakra: *Power. Just above the navel. The ability to have a say in your life. Ability to be effective in the world; to say "yes" when you mean yes, and "no" when you mean no. How to assert your will.*

The surest way to restore balance in the Third Chakra is practice some self-discipline. In small ways or big ways, demonstrate some self-control. Establish a healthy schedule and stick to it; set some goals for yourself, or initiate a fitness routine; practice restraint somewhere in your life just to demonstrate to yourself that you can! Effectiveness begins at home, and when you begin to focus more on self-control than expressing frustration with events or others, the illusion that life is all competition disappears.

Fourth Chakra

When all three of the lower chakras are balanced, the energy naturally rises to the Fourth Chakra, the heart. This is both a quantum leap and a qualitative shift of where you direct your attention. You rise above petty issues and experience the joy of deep acceptance. From the Awakened Heart, life no longer seems threatening, nor a struggle. Competition gives way to cooperation. Anxiety gives way to tranquility. Hostility gives way to love. Whether it is experienced as personal love, compassionate love, or universal love, it is always unconditional. You have learned how to tap into a source of love that is not dependent on circumstances, or how others treat you.

The Heart Chakra is the first of the upper chakras where you can tap into universal energy. When you are sharing and giving from the Awakened Heart, the love comes through you; you are tapping into the universal, inexhaustible source and you will not experience the burnout and exhaustion that comes from personal giving.

When imbalances occur with any of the upper chakras, the cause is most likely in the lower chakras, deflecting the true course of the chakra in question. In the case of the Heart Chakra, troubles in love have the sources in the lower chakras. When the lower chakras interfere with the true nature of unconditional love, "I love you" translates as "I need you," or "I desire you," or "I seek to control you." To balance these issues, go to the chakra in question, restore balance with the issues of security, pleasure, or power that are disrupting your heart.

Even with compassion, "I suffer for you" brings it all back to the "I," the realm of the lower chakras. The separate "I" melts with the Awakened Heart, and it becomes possible to gently touch suffering with loving-kindness and not carry the suffering with you. Grasping and aversion both pull us out of our center. A teacher once said, "Joy is a function of immense acceptance." This certainly refers to an Awakened Heart. To stay centered in your heart, practice deep acceptance by dropping all judgments of self and others. Even excessive humility ("I'm not worthy") and despair ("Woe is me") are still "I" and "me" focused. When judgment happens, note it and realize this is the voice of the lower chakras, and simply decide not to listen to the judgment, not to empower it in any way. This helps you to literally rise above the petty voices and stay centered in your loving and accepting heart.

Fourth Chakra: *Love. At the heart. Dropping all feelings of separateness and feeling connected to the world. Deep appreciation and compassion for others.*

Fifth Chakra

As the energy rises to the Fifth Chakra at the throat, you awaken to original insights and are able to creatively express yourself in a way that is not conditioned by culture or others. You find your true voice. This is the mind, but not limited to the ego-encapsulated view of life, you are liberated to explore the universal mind itself. Your ability to express yourself creatively comes from this access to the source of all human creativity.

An example demonstrating that the Fifth Chakra is collective and not personal is illustrated in the following scenario. You get a creative inspiration, but, for one reason or another, fail to act on it. What happens? Somebody else writes your book, or your play, or comes up with the invention, or acts on the original insight that you thought was yours. Creativity is a *collective* resource; if you don't act on your creative inspirations, somebody else will.

Fifth Chakra: ***Creativity. At the throat. The need to express your truth. Access to the universal mind; flashes, insights, and sudden knowing. Sudden surges of mental energy.***

Liberating yourself from all cultural conditioning facilitates the awakening of your Fifth Chakra. You must be willing to question all of your existing beliefs, and even if you reincorporate beliefs you received from your culture, this first must come from deep questioning. Those who are able to sustain Fifth Chakra level of awareness are universal in their perspective of truth. By rising out of your own conditioning, you are able to see the beauty behind many religions, beliefs, and political views. You become like an evolutionary agent for your culture, and your insights serve as a catalyst for others to question their views as well.

There is a nervous type of energy that accompanies the Fifth Chakra opening. When you try to quell this energy, it is experienced as nervous anxiety; when you align with it, it is experienced as a quickening. Imbalances in the Fifth Chakra, like writer's block, or the inability to speak up in a group, or stage fright, all stem from the ego inappropriately identifying with energy it can't control. Keep the ego out of it to allow the Fifth Chakra to operate at its best.

If you are experiencing writer's block, shift your attention from your frustration to the needs of the audience you are addressing and watch the information get pulled out of you. If you suffer from stage fright, note that all of your attention is on the increased energy you feel and your assessment that you shouldn't be feeling it. You can't stop the energy, it comes with the situation; everyone in the audience is focusing their attention on you giving you *their* energy. You can't stop the energy, but you can quit evaluating it and thinking it shouldn't be there. Accept it and offer it back to the audience, and you will give the most exciting, dynamic, innovative speech of your life.

Sixth Chakra

The Sixth Chakra is located behind the brow, just above the bridge of your nose. As the energy rises to the Sixth Chakra, the third eye is awakened and inner vision is born, with imagination being its mode of expression. The ability to see with your eyes closed, to imagine experiences that are not available to your normal sensory world—this is truly a gift. From the Sixth Chakra perspective, you rise above all polarity in your life and see a larger reality that encompasses all duality. This is the home of the witness point in consciousness, which can observe self in action. You are in the world but not of the world, thus you do not get pulled into polarities.

This is the realm of the angels, ascended beings, the flow of the Tao, the Big Sky Mind, and the still, quiet voice within; experiences from here are always inspirational. When you are aligned with the Sixth Chakra, your faith in the source beyond self is empowered by direct experience, and a sense of "knowing" beyond mental concepts comes over you.

When the pure witnessing of the balanced Sixth Chakra is interfered with by the desires and fears of the ego, this spiritual faculty gets deflected to the ego's needs, and then imagination can lead to escapism, drugs, alcohol, deception, and illusions of all sorts. All of these delusions are the workings of the imagination, too, but with these expressions there is always a depletion of your energy. When the imagination is linked to creative, mystical, and spiritual sources, your energy field is always enhanced.

Sixth Chakra: ***Inspiration. At the brow. Transcendence. Access to spiritual and psychic realms. The ability to imagine, leading to inspirations or illusions.***

Whether it was inspiration or illusion that you were listening to is always evident retrospectively. It is only too clear after the fact.

To catch your imagination in the moment and notice if it is moving toward inspiration or illusion is subtle work, but profound. If I asked you to take notice of your general energy field while you are reading this passage, you could easily do this, and note if you were feeling inspired, tired, agitated, etc. The place within you that is doing the noticing is known as "the Witness." The trick is to do this very same assessment while in the state of imagination.

To work with your Sixth Chakra, you need to know that fear and faith are flip sides of the same coin. They are both fueled by the imagination. Fear and faith are the same energy, true, but radically different in their impact on your energy field. When you hear a noise outside your room and fear it might be an intruder, your energy field responds very different than if you imagined the noise to be a reminder from your guardian angel. It takes your spiritual will to: (1) stay observant to whether your imagination is moving toward fear or faith; and (2) to extract your attention from negative wanderings and direct it to that which inspires you.

Easy enough to talk about, but when you are imagining, you have transcended the place within you that can remember to do this exercise! You have to stay mindful of being in two places simultaneously within yourself. You are involved in the imagination, and at the same time, aware of the Witness and its ability to observe the experience and its impact on your energy field. It may be slight, but discernable. Take note: Is there a subtle enhancement or depletion of your energy field? Is there a feeling of opening and expansiveness? Or is there a tightness, restriction, or a heavy feeling? Does it feel like your energy is being drained? These are the clues that you can train yourself to use to distinguish between inspiration and illusion in the moment. Now it is up to your spiritual will to extract your attention from Sixth Chakra wanderings that are not empowering and direct it toward the source that fills you with inspiration.

Seventh Chakra

When the energy rises to the crown of the head and the Seventh Chakra, you become absorbed into God Consciousness. Called the "thousand-petalled lotus blossom," because it represents the flowering of human consciousness at its highest expression, its roots are deep in the muck of reality. At the Crown Chakra, all sense of separate identity dissolves into the vast oneness. Only a handful of saints and masters have been able to sustain this level of consciousness, while for most of us, there will only be a few glimpses of this reality in an entire lifetime. Psychologists have talked of "peak," or "oceanic," experiences that, although rare, often mark major transitions in a person's life. These openings of the Seventh Chakra are glimpses of life through God's eyes.

Seventh Chakra: *Spiritual. At the crown of the head. Absolute union with the Divine. Experiences of Divine awareness.*

Seventh Chakra experiences are ineffable; they can't be described. "The Tao that can be told is not the eternal Tao."[9] This is the realm of Samadhi, enlightenment, and God-centered consciousness. If you are so blessed as to receive a few of these illuminating experiences in this life, don't try to understand them with your mind, just be thankful that you have been so blessed. To open to this energy, practice quieting your mind and noticing the God force that is all around you. Open to this Divine energy and picture receiving it into your being through your Crown Chakra.

Disruptions from the Lower Chakras

As mentioned previously, the first three chakras are the most likely culprits of imbalances. They are grasping and self-serving by nature, which is needed for self-preservation, but if attention is exclusively focused here, life seems competitive and threatening. The lower chakras are not bad; that's not the point. It is when they're not in harmony with the whole system that problems develop. An example would be when the drives and needs of the lower chakras exclusively dominate your awareness, effectively blocking you from experiencing higher levels of consciousness. Another example would be when the ego operates outside of its natural turf of the first three chakras, and puts a personal spin on something that wasn't meant to be personal. The upper chakras awaken us to spiritual levels of consciousness, beyond the ego's grasp. When you awaken to upper chakra experiences and put a personal spin on them, again, problems would develop.

A common example occurs when you awaken to your Fourth Chakra level of universal love and try to make it personal. There is a personal level of love with the awakened Fourth Chakra that is shared with loved ones, but there is also a universal level of love that can feel this same Awakened Heart with so many others. This can be confusing when you feel a soul connection and deep love for someone outside of your commitment circle. When the Heart Chakra is awakened, there is a tremendous outpouring of the heart. It would be easy for you, or someone else, to interpret this as personal and try to form a relationship around it. To stay in the Awakened Heart, you need to let go of analyzing the love and trying to make it "fit" in your life. Let it be without evaluation or needing to act on it. Remember that the lower chakras try to make everything personal, to figure out what's in this for you.

It is not about repressing the needs of any of the chakras; not at all. It is awakening to each of them individually, and balancing all of their needs within the entire system as well. The chakras teach us that we are all multidimensional beings; there is more going on than is first apparent.

As we bring the lower chakras into balance, we most naturally awaken to love, compassion, creativity, insight, psychic sensitivity, and spiritual guidance from the still, quiet voice within. As the teaching goes, it is not so much achieving enlightenment, as it is removing the blocks that stand in its way.

A Chakra Meditation

Sit in a comfortable meditation position with your spine straight. Make certain that your head is directly over your shoulders and not slouched forward. You can imagine a cord attached to the crown of your head that is gently pulling you upward. Breathe a few deep breaths to center yourself.

Now imagine the color red in your mind's eye. Any shade of red that comes to you will work. Imagine breathing in this color on a deep in-breath. Bring it all the way down to your tailbone. As you hold your breath, focus your attention on your First Chakra and picture the red energy animating your being. Imagine the chakra as a wheel of red light, spinning and radiating and filling you with this color. Feel the courage and strength of red animate your animal nature. Here you are a creature of nature, part of the animal kingdom. Feel the aliveness of your body and imagine being someplace on Earth where your body absolutely feels its best. Here, you can trust your instincts for survival, and trust that you will be safe and cared for on the Earth this day. Feel the security come over you; empower your First Chakra with trust.

Now imagine any shade of orange that comes to your mind. Breathe in orange and pull it down to your Second Chakra, just above the pubic bone. As you focus on your Second Chakra, picture this spinning and radiating orange light. Feel the joy, the warmth, and the pleasure of awakening your Second Chakra. Know that you are a magnetic being and can attract to you all you need and want. As you breathe out, send this joyous, magnetic energy out into the world.

Next, it is yellow and the Third Chakra. Again, find the shade of yellow that you are drawn to, breathe this color into your Third Chakra, just above your navel. As you breathe into your solar plexus, see the chakra begin to spin and radiate yellow. Feel the power of your will, and know that you can use your will wisely. From here you can initiate activities and define your boundaries. Feel the confidence that comes from having self-control, and knowing you can say "yes" when you mean yes, and "no" when you mean no.

On to the Fourth Chakra and the color green. Find a shade of green that calls to you in your mind's eye, and breathe this color into your Heart Chakra, in the middle of your chest. Set the chakra spinning and radiating a green light that fills your entire being. Rest in the healing energy of green. The Heart Chakra is the "Heaven on Earth" place; the meeting place of the lower and upper chakras. Feel the deep peace, joy, love, and compassion that arise with this awakening. When you look at others from your heart, you do not see their personality traits; you see another soul in a human incarnation struggling to be free. Compassion, empathy, and contentment are also experiences you can awaken to while centered in the Heart Chakra. It is particularly important to offer these experiences of love into the world. Establish the high intent of offering any good that comes from your meditation out into the world, so that it may be helpful to others.

Next move on to the Fifth Chakra and the color sky blue. Imagine looking up at the bright, blue sky. Breathe into this blue and pull it down to the base of your spine. As this blue rises up the spine, feel yourself becoming elongated, as if there was a puff of air between each of your vertebrae as this sky blue journeys upward. Focus the blue on your Throat Chakra and set the chakra spinning in your mind's eye. Feel yourself become as expansive as the sky. Here, your thoughts become clear, unclouded by desires, or the opinions of others. Here, you breathe the same air that has animated all creative genius. Here, you can speak the truth that does not need to be defended. Feel the freedom of your liberated mind as it sails into the sky far removed from personal opinions; yours or others. Pledging your intention to wanting to somehow be helpful for others with information you might receive, be open to sudden knowing.

The Sixth Chakra and deep indigo blue come next. Imagine the color of the furthest reaches of the Earth's atmosphere just before it turns black. Breathe this color into your third eye, just above the bridge of your nose. Again, imagine the chakra spinning and radiating this deepest of blue light. Imagine yourself rising into the deep blue atmosphere above Earth and looking back at Earth from the same view as we see from the space shuttle. Feel the transcendence of this view. Your view is so far removed that you can't even see individual lives, only the Earth and her continents, oceans, and weather. Feel the bliss of this transcendence. Allow the sacredness of the moment to wash over you. To stay centered here requires a quieting of the analyzing voice. Just listen and observe. Thinking will happen, but pay it no mind; let the thoughts come and go as you stay anchored in the Sixth Chakra, just observing. Surrender to any devotional feelings for teachers, masters, and saints that may come over you spontaneously while you are meditating on your Sixth Chakra. Find the place of trust and faith that all of life is unfolding as it should.

The Seventh Chakra and the color violet complete the meditation. This is the most spiritual chakra and your connection to that which is most high. Imagine a violet flame over your head. Picture it a deep violet where it touches your head, and as it rises upward into the heavens, picture it becoming increasingly more ultraviolet and then invisible. Breathe deep into this spiritual flame and pull it down to the base of your spine. Picture it cleansing and purifying each chakra as it passes through. Picture the violet flame rising through each of your chakras and ultimately out your crown and up to the heavens. Focus your attention on your crown chakra and affirm, "I am a child of God." Know that beyond all illusions and appearances you have a direct connection to God within. Here resides Atman, the eternal self, who has never been wounded nor bruised by life. Feel as if you are being absorbed back into the one.

The Sushumna, Kundalini, Ida, and Pingala

The sushumna is shown in the illustration as a hollow tube connecting the chakras to one another. *Kundalini,* meaning "coiled serpent," is a vast reserve of energy at the base of the spine. Through body postures, pranayama, and meditation, the yogi raises the kundalini energy up the sushumna to further animate each chakra. The ida and pingala are the main trunks of the subtle energy system, called the *nadis* that branch throughout the entire body. By consciously withdrawing prana from the ida and pingala and redirecting this prana to the base of the spine and the sushumna, the kundalini energy is made to rise up the sushumna animating each successive chakra.

In Patanjali's Eight Limbs of Yoga, Pratyahara, the process of consciously withdrawing attention from the senses, is the fifth step. The above method is a technique for consciously withdrawing sensory attention, by cutting it off at the roots, the ida and pingala.

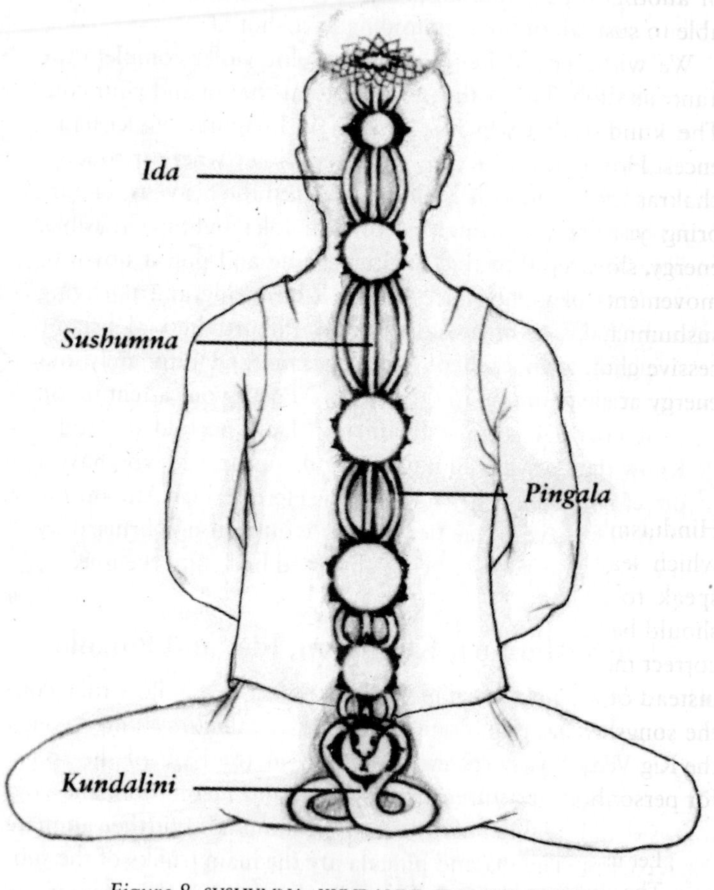

Figure 8. SUSHUMNA, KUNDALINI, IDA, AND PINGALA.

When a person has a spontaneous kundalini experience, unawares and unexpected, he awakens to energy he can't handle, and it is anything but pleasant. But for the person with knowledge and training, this awakened energy is the elixir of life. The energy can be sustained when it is balanced. Without balance the increased energy will seek to be grounded through some dramatic event. The energy builds, but seeks to fire off like a spark plug to go back to a more comfortable level of energy. An argument, power conflict, huge struggle of one type or another, or lust are all possible manifestations of not being able to sustain increased energy.

We will discuss the kundalini and sexuality further in the Tantra section (see page 169), but it has direct application here. The kundalini spontaneously awakens during sexual experiences. However, if not coaxed upward, it will stay in the lower chakras, and the increased energy will fire off as an orgasm to bring you back to more comfortable levels. To sustain the energy, slow down the rush to orgasm, literally slow down body movements, and imagine the kundalini energy rising in the sushumna. As you imagine the kundalini awakening each successive chakra, picture your energy merging with your partner's energy at each level.

The Sacred Texts of Hinduism

Hinduism's sacred texts are written in a lyrical, poetic style, which leaves much room for individual interpretation. They speak to different people in different ways, and this is as it should be. There is no final authority, no definitive word on its correct meaning. This allows a reader to gain firsthand insights, instead of attempting to learn the correct meaning. They speak the songs of the soul, spirit, and God. The Gaitri mantra, from the Rig Veda, is an excellent example of the simplicity and room for personal experience of the Hindu scriptures:

> Let us bring our minds to rest in
> The glory of Divine Truth.
> May Truth inspire our reflection.[10]

The Vedas

The Vedas are considered to be the original sacred texts that all of Hinduism has grown from. The Vedas are a compilation of many writings over a vast period of time, beginning approximately 1,500 B.C.E. The most influential of these are the Rig Veda, the oldest of the texts, and the Upanishads, the final addition to the Vedas. It is commonly believed that the original Vedas were revealed knowledge, as opposed to created by man. The original Vedas were a written form of what had been an ongoing oral tradition for who knows how long. The Rig Veda is a beautiful volume of songs of praise to God and Creation. Within the chants and mantras of the Rig Veda, the Hindu cosmology is revealed and they teach the sacred interconnectedness of all life.

The original language of the Vedas is Sanskrit, the holy language. Translations can only hint to Sanskrit meanings. Sanskrit is thought to be an intentional language, the sound of a word itself carries a vibration that triggers the appropriate physical, emotional, mental and spiritual responses; you get it at many levels simultaneously.

However, Sanskrit was a language only the Brahmins knew, thus affording them the highest ranking in the hierarchy of Indian culture. It wasn't until the epics of the Bhagavad Gita and the Ramayana popularized the teachings and made them available for all to interpret that the Brahmins lost this lofty place in Hindu culture. The Vedas, however, have never lost their place of deep reverence among Hindus.

The Upanishads

The Upanishads are formally part of the Vedas, but deserve consideration as a stand-alone body of spiritual knowledge. The Upanishads are commentaries on the original Vedas, which were composed sometime between the ninth and third century B.C.E. It is not known how many original Upanishads there were, perhaps over 100, but ever since Shankara decreed that ten of these were the most significant, so it has been. Where the original Vedas present the rituals and hymns for connecting with the gods, the Upanishads focus on the internalization of the teachings. They map out the inner states of consciousness in exquisite detail, revealing that all of it is illusionary and only Brahman-Atman is real.

Upanishad means "sitting down near," and these writings are said to be of the direct transmissions from the teacher to the student. What is the meaning of life? Of death? Is there an ultimate reality? Is there a God? These perennial questions of all seekers are directly addressed. The ten teachings present the method for full awakening to Atman, the Self, in this life. Written in lyrical style, they play upon your soul and give a fresh insight with each reading.

The Bhagavad Gita

The Bhagavad Gita is revered by Hindus. It is fairly short and can be read in an afternoon, yet many study it for a lifetime of spiritual guidance. Originally written as part of a larger epic, The Mahabharata, near the middle of the first millennium B.C.E., the "Gita" was added much later, and, as a stand-alone piece of literature, is considered to be one of the holiest of sacred texts.

The story unfolds as a dialogue between Arjuna and Lord Krishna. Arjuna is a great warrior about to go into battle. He stops to consider his actions with his charioteer who, unbeknownst to him, is Lord Krishna himself. Many of the core teachings of Hinduism are revealed through their dialogue.

Arjuna stops because he sees relatives and people he knows in the opposing army, and wonders if he would be creating karma for himself by killing those he knows and respects. It is then that the charioteer reveals himself as Krishna and instructs Arjuna to follow his dharma, his natural path of being a warrior, and to dedicate all of his actions to God.

Hindus are not literalists and take this teaching at two levels. On the one hand, it seems to support the path of Karma Yoga, and dedicating the merit to God. But the story is also looked at symbolically. The family members and known ones that Arjuna is encouraged to slay are the lower voices within his own ego—pride, envy, anger, desire all are known, but must be slain. The great battle is within for the spiritual warrior.

Throughout the Gita, Krishna provides Arjuna with spiritual instruction. In their dialogue, the way of the yogis is expounded upon. While many paths to God are discussed, particular attention is paid to the path of Karma Yoga.

Although he acknowledges the Sankhya, Krishna teaches the path of action, of Karma Yoga, is higher because no one, even for an instant, remains really actionless; such is the nature of the reality we are born to. Even choosing to not act is an action. Krishna tells Arjuna that karma is not created by actions, but instead by the emotional responses to actions. If one can remain detached and dedicate all activity to God, one becomes free of negative karma.

In Buddhism, dharma was described as the teachings of the Buddha. In Hinduism, dharma refers to one's natural essence, or the role you came here to play. By staying true to your essence and not attempting to be something you aren't, by finding the type of work and service in the world that honors your true nature, being of service to others and constantly being aware of the Divine, you are following your dharma path of Karma Yoga.

Dharma: ***In Buddhism, dharma was described as the teachings of the Buddha. In Hinduism, dharma refers to one's natural essence, or the role you came here to play.***

The Ramayana

This great epic story of the love between Rama and Sita is cherished as a holy text by Hindus. It is said to have been written by the legendary saint Valmiki, in the fourth century B.C.E. It could easily said to be authored by the whole culture as it was continually molded and revised over the next centuries. It illuminates the teachings of Hinduism in a popular love story that is still revered by Hindus today. It is acted out in plays and dances that never fail to enthrall the audience. In Bali, there is at least one performance of the Ramayana weekly.

The story portrays Rama's royal life as a prince, revealing him to be one of the incarnations of Vishnu in human form, and then falling in love with Sita. A dark lord, Ravana, captures Sita, and Rama seeks the help of the monkey king, Hanuman, who with his monkey army liberates Sita. There are further trials for the immortal couple. Rama begins to doubt Sita's loyalty and she is banished from the kingdom. Their reuniting, ultimate death, and becoming gods is further portrayed.

Along with the Bhagavad Gita, the Ramayana liberated the sacred teachings from the exclusive hold of the Brahmins, and did much to expand the appeal of Hinduism.

The Puranas

This is the sacred literature of those on the Bhakti path. There are eighteen main Puranas, which are an important storehouse of Hindu mythology. These writings carry much of the mythology, the genealogy, rites, rituals, songs, and sacred sites of Hinduism. This further expanded Hinduism's reach into society. They date as far back as the sixth century C.E. for the oldest of writings, and most of them from the twelfth and thirteenth century C.E.

The Tantra Tradition

Although we will not be going into the subject here, the Tantric tradition is also an important aspect of Hinduism and should at least be mentioned. Since both Hinduism and Buddhism embrace Tantra teachings, it will be explored in its own separate chapter (see page 169).

After Thoughts

For thousands of years, Hinduism has been mapping out the distinct levels of consciousness of the subconscious, conscious, dreaming, and transcendent realms that we in the West have only recently become aware of with the "discoveries" of Freud, just one hundred years ago.

—David Pond

"Love says I am everything. Wisdom says I am nothing. Between the two my life flows. . . ."

—Nisargadatta Maharaj

To know that it is an illusion that any of these waves is truly separate from the ocean is wisdom; to take delight in the beauty of each wave is love; and between the two is Leela, the play of consciousness.

—David Pond

It's all an illusion, it's all real; to be attached to neither and to be able to move between the two is freedom.

—David Pond

Individual thoughts rise up out of the mind, demand attention as if they are real, and collapse back into the oneness of life.

—David Pond

Individual lives unfold from the ocean of emptiness, demand attention as if they are real and collapse back into the emptiness.

—David Pond

This great freedom of knowing the truth of who you are releases you from the confines of separateness and allows you to embrace the source behind self.

—David Pond

Suggested Reading

Besant, Annie (translator). *The Bhagavad Gita.* Adyar, Madras: The Theosophical Publishing House, 1914.

Bhaskarananda, Swami. *The Essentials of Hinduism.* Seattle, Wash.: Viveka Press, 1994.

Cross, Steven. *Hinduism.* Rockport, Mass.: Element Books, 1994.

Easwaran, Eknath. *Thousand Names of Vishnu.* Berkeley, Calif.: Nilgiri Press, 1987.

———. *The Bhagavad Gita.* Berkeley, Calif.: Nilgiri Press, 1985.

———. *Meditation.* Berkeley, Calif.: Nilgiri Press, 1987.

———. *The Upanishads.* Berkeley, Calif.: The Blue Mountain Center for Meditation, 1987.

Hari Dass, Baba. *The Yoga Sutras of Patanjali.* Santa Cruz, Calif.: SRI Rama Publishing, 1999.

Hayes, Peter. *The Supreme Adventure.* New York, N.Y.: Delta, 1988.

Iyengar, B.K.S. *Light on the Yoga Sutras of Patanjali.* San Francisco, Calif.: Aquarian Press, 1993.

Le Mee, Jean. *Hymns from the Rig-Veda.* New York, N.Y.: Alfred A. Knopf, 1975.

Muktananda, Baba. *Play of Consciousness.* California: Shree Gurudev Siddha Yoga Ashram, 1974.

Osborne, Arthur. *Ramana Maharshi and the Path of Self-Knowledge.* York Beach, Maine: Samuel Weiser, 1970.

Nikhilananda, Swami (translator) *The Gospel of Sri Ramakrishna.* New York: Ramakrishna-Vivekananda Center, 1942.

Nisargatta, Maharaj. *I Am That.* Durham, North Carolina: Acorn Press, 1973.

Prabhavananda, Swami. *The Spiritual Heritage of India.* Hollywood: Vedanta Press, 1979.

Shakti Parwha Kaur Khalsa. *Kundalini Yoga.* New York: Perigree Books, 1996.

Vishnudevananda, Swami. *The Complete Illustrated Book of Yoga.* New York: Bell Publishing Co., 1960.

Vivekananda, Swami. *Raja-Yoga.* New York: Ramakrishna-Vivekananda Center, 1956.

Yogananda, Paramahansa. *Autobiography of a Yogi.* New York, N.Y.: Philosophical Library, 1946.

Yukteswar, Sri. *The Holy Science.* Los Angeles: Self-Realization Fellowship, 1972.

The Encyclopedia of Eastern Philosophy and Religion. Boston, Mass.: Shambhala, 1989.

Endnotes

1. Le Mee, Jean, translator. *Hymns from the Rig Veda.* p. 216.
2. Yogananda. *Autobiography of a Yogi.* pp. 14, 17–18, 88–90.
3. Cross, Stephen. *Hinduism.* p. 64.
4. Osborne, Arthur. *Ramana Maharshi and the Path of Self-Knowledge.* pp. 18–19.
5. Nikhilananda, Swami (translator). *The Gospel of Sri Ramakrishna.* pp. 119–120.
6. Yukteswar, Sri. *The Holy Science.* pp. viii–xviv.
7. Yogananda. *Autobiography of a Yogi.* p. 120.
8. Hari Dass, Baba. *The Yoga Sutras of Patanjali.* p. 5.
9. Mitchell, Stephen. *Tao Te Ching.* p. 1.
10. Le Mee, Jean, translator. *Hymns from the Rig Veda.* p. 4.

TAOISM

Are you the sort of person who finds more spiritual fulfillment from a walk in nature than you do from any type of church experience? If so, perhaps you are a Taoist at heart. Nature speaks deep truth to the Taoist. Taoism is the practice of aligning with the mysterious Tao—the Way—which is most readily revealed through nature. It is taught that there is an inherent natural order in the universe, and the movement, the flow of this natural order, which pervades all of existence, is the Tao.

Humans live out their lives within this grand scheme as nothing more, or less, special than any other aspect of creation. The individual person is part of the vast matrix of the Tao, not more important, not less important than the tree, the rock, or the frog. This leads to a philosophy of aligning with the way of nature and cultivating attitudes of gentleness, openness, and disappearing from conflict. To live in alignment with the Tao is to have a deep faith that your needs will be amply provided for by totally surrendering to a path of living in harmony with each moment.

All things come from the Tao, and by aligning with it, your life begins to unfold effortlessly and your true path is revealed. However, there is nothing that can be done to make this happen. There are no special skills to develop, nor is any particular talent required. This is the mystery of the Tao; it can't be attained. It comes from deep acceptance; accepting that the Tao is not going to be revealed in any moment other than here and now. The past is memory, the future just thought, it is only in this present moment that one can live in alignment with the Tao, and trusting in this is "the Way."

From the simple teaching of aligning with the Way, a whole spiritual system has been born. There is not just one form of Taoism; there are many. Philosophical and contemplative Taoism focuses on the teachings as a way of living, and this is where we will focus most in this chapter. For many, Taoism is the basis of intense discipline, and the teachings have fueled major developments in the fields of martial arts, Chi Kung, health, hygiene, and inner discovery. Taoist sexual teachings have added to the world knowledge on the role of sexuality in health, vitality, longevity, and, for some, the quest for immortality.

All of these traditions claim allegiance to the Tao and use nature as the great teacher. There are branches of Taoism that rival the complexity of Hinduism, but the core teachings of aligning with truth revealed through nature appeal to those who resist the rigid structure of many religions. This leads to a key distinction between Taoism and Hinduism. Hinduism teaches transcendence of the physical world as the ideal, whereas Taoism embraces a deep interaction with nature as the highest path. Tao, God, the universal life force, is not going to be found in some other reality other than right here, right now.

The Tao Te Ching

The formal roots of Taoism can be traced to a simple book of just over 5,000 words, *Tao Te Ching* (pronounced "Dao De Ching") by Lao Tzu, written in approximately 550 B.C.E. The book cannot be improved on by commentary, and is a must-read for all seekers. In terms of sheer elegance of style, the *Tao Te Ching* is a treasure of artistic magnitude. In terms of a book of wisdom, again it is unsurpassed in its profound truths, presented with grace and simplicity.

The title consists of three words. *Tao* is "the Way," *Te* is translated both as "virtue" and "power," and *Ching* simply means "book," and more specifically, a "classic." Thus, the title translates as "The Book of the Way and its Virtues," or "The Book of the Way and its Power." Tao is the constant flow of life and its many cycles, patterns, and rhythms. Te is the manifesting power of this when one aligns with the Way. When you are right with yourself and the Tao, your life works because it is your natural Te for it to do so.

Written in poetic form and filled with paradox, the eighty-one poems that make up the book are clearly not intended to be intellectual dogma of any sort. The opening stanza states, "The Tao that can be told is not the eternal Tao." The book starts off negating even its own attempts to describe the Tao and points to another way of perceiving that is not mental, rational, nor logical. One must drop into the feeling nature to align with the Tao, as it must be discovered anew by each person in each moment.

Heady philosophical elaboration of the teachings of the Tao would be like using a computer to analyze art—the wrong tool. This approach would miss the whole artistic sensitivity and feeling transmitted through the artwork. This is like the mind analyzing nature; it will miss the whole feeling component if you let it. And so it is with the Tao. It is not mental whatsoever; it must be felt.

From the #56 of the Tao:

> Those who know do not talk
> Those who talk do not know.[1]

This is not because the Tao is occult and must be kept secret; it is because the Tao is not of the realm of words. You have to develop a feel for the Tao; no rules apply. Those who find comfort with set rules and beliefs will find no comfort with the Tao. You must access a deeper knowledge other than that which normally makes sense. Although the colloquialism "go with the flow" has somewhat trivialized the concept, still the intent of the statement captures the attitude of the Tao.

Lao Tzu

The life of Lao Tzu, author of the *Tao Te Ching,* has been difficult for scholars to authenticate—whether he was real, legendary, or a composite is up for debate. There seems to be no record of his birth, so even exact dating is difficult. It appears that he was born near the end of the fifth century B.C.E. and was said to be an elder contemporary of Confucius, which also places him in the same era as Shakyamuni Buddha.

Legend has it that he held an unassuming job working with the imperial archives. Not much is known about his life until his retirement when he prepares to leave China through the western region and is somehow recognized by the guard at the gate as a person of great wisdom. The guard persuades Lao Tzu to delay his journey for one night and write down some of his wisdom before departing. Lao Tzu obliges him, and the *Tao Te Ching* is born as his offering.

Just as before this scene at the gate, little is known about Lao Tzu's later life. He seems to disappear and apparently goes on about his retirement—however, to this day, the *Tao Te Ching* continues to inspire millions of seekers worldwide. The founding father of the *Tao Te Ching* left no footprints. Even his birth records have been obscured by the winds of time, and there is something altogether invisible about the man. So consistent with his teachings; we know him by his works, while he remains invisible!

As Lao Tzu says in #27 of the *Tao:* "A good traveler leaves no track or trace."[2]

The Way

The Way of the Tao is most often compared to the nature of water. It sustains life without effort or judgment, nurturing weeds and flowers alike; water always flows with the path of least resistance; if it comes to an obstacle, it goes around it; if water comes to a hole, it first fills it up and then continues on its way. Water always adapts to its environment, yet remains true to its own identity. Water can be liquid, solid, or vapor, depending on conditions. This is the Way; yielding, responding and adapting, but always being true to your essential identity. Not contemplating the past, nor considering the future, instead, adapting to the eternal now.

God in Taoism

Tao is God in Taoism; both transcendent (it can't be named) and imminent (Tao is the mother of all things and in all things). This is an impersonal God, the creator of everything, but not its ruler.

From #51:

Tao produces them (ten thousand things)
 but does not take possession of them.
It acts, but does not rely on its own ability.
It leads them but does not master them.
This is called Profound and secret Virtue.[3]

From #5:

The Tao doesn't take sides;
It gives birth to both good and evil.
The Master doesn't take sides;
She welcomes both sinners and saints.

The Tao is like a bellows;
It is empty, yet infinitely capable.
The more you use it,
The more it produces;
The more you talk of it, the less you understand
Hold on to the center.[4]

These two sutras reveal Tao to be the mother of all creation and indiscriminate in her love, like rain, which falls on both the moral and the wicked. It's there to be drawn upon like the bellows, yet it doesn't demand use or allegiance. An arsonist or artist could use the bellows; it is not moralistic about who can draw on it.

This lackadaisical attitude about morals concerns many. "Without moral training, how would a child know how to be good?" some may ask. The Taoist view doesn't turn its back on this and ignore the issue. It is taught that when you align with your true nature and are in harmony with your life, others have their best chance of aligning to their true nature, which is also in harmony with life—not because it should be so, instead because it simply is so. The best you can do for others is to live in alignment with the Tao yourself.

The simplest way to align with the Taoist concept of God is to see the sacred, the Tao, in all things including self.

The Expression of Te

If it is all Tao, what makes a tree a tree and you who you are, different from the tree? Te. *Te* is often translated as "virtue" and this hints of moral training as in virtuous. Te is much more than this. Here virtue is used as in properties, i.e. a particular herb's healing properties are its virtues (and its power). It is the manifesting principle behind Tao; what makes a thing what it is. Te is also translated as "power;" the power that comes from living the Way. Everything in life has a pattern that allows it to become what it is. By aligning with the Tao, your natural patterning expression of Te has its best chance to manifest.

When you follow your true nature, the pattern works because it is in its nature to do so. This takes a bit of faith. Taoism is not big on philosophy and thinking through each situation. It is placing complete faith in the eternal now and honoring the Tao within you at this moment, trusting the manifesting power of Te will have no difficulty providing for your needs. You are part of the same fabric and sustained by the same force as all of nature. A tree doesn't have to work at becoming a tree—it is in its nature to do so. So it is with your true nature—you do not have to work at becoming your true nature; it is already within you.

The importance of Te is expressed in this passage from Chuang-Tzu's delightful commentaries on Taoism from the third century B.C.E.

> When a man has perfect virtue (Te), fire cannot burn him,
> water cannot drown him, cold and heat cannot afflict him,
> birds and beasts cannot injure him.[5]

This powerful claim means that if you were in touch with your true nature and a tree was about to fall on you, just before it happened you would have been led to get up and move, maybe to get a drink of water, or to use the bathroom, but one way or another to not be where the danger falls.

This teaching substantiates faith in the Way. When you are in touch with your true nature and in harmony with life, you are aligned with both Te and Tao. Aligning with the Tao has the benefits of increased tranquility in your life, but it also has built-in safety measures. Since all of life is interconnected, if danger is approaching from any direction, the Tao would lead you to safety, even before the threat.

If the Tao is everywhere, including within you, then the Divine presence is being manifest through you as all others. When you fall out of alignment with the Tao, it becomes self-perpetuating. When you get into negative spaces, you send out negative energy and attract the circumstances that support the worry, fear, or doubt. The all-manifesting Tao is within you as well, so if your divine statement is "I am worried about . . ." "I am fearful of . . ." then the manifesting power of Te is deflected to support your essentially false image.

Examine your "I Am" statement throughout the day. Whatever you are focusing on, that is your "I Am" statement and what you are giving your life force to, and most certainly that which will manifest.

As easy and beautiful as this philosophy is, it takes tremendous self-affirmation to follow this path. You can't follow the Tao by consensus thinking and trying to fit into your culture. You have to let go of all social "shoulds" and honor your own intrinsic truth. This cannot be found by following social dictates, it has to be found within, and it is inherently there. The energy blueprint of Te and its formative power is within you in your most natural state. To align with your Te takes deep acceptance, not ambition.

This lack of ambition, however, should not be confused with complacency. And it is certainly not self-denial in any way—quite the contrary. To accept the Tao is everywhere implies the Divine force is equally within you as it is in all things. Obviously, you could not awaken to this by self-denial. Accepting the greatness of all embracing Tao within is not meant to be ego enhancing, but is certainly not self-denial. The "I" is Divine because the Tao is Divine, and Tao is in all things.

Imagine that you are a cell within your body. How would your needs be met? You would not need to learn how to fulfill your role; it would be inherent within the Te of the cell to naturally do so. Since it is in the body's best interest that the cell fulfills its function, the body will naturally provide for all of the cell's needs. It is in the body's best interest to do so. The cell would not become more secure by defending against the rest of the body—exactly the opposite. The cell doesn't even need to know that it needs oxygen, blood, and nutrients. The body knows and it is inherent that it supplies all of these needs. If the cell is in alignment with the Tao of the body, all of its needs will be met.

We could carry this further and say that the Taoist cell wouldn't be concerned with why it is a cell, or if it will be a cell in the afterlife, or next life. Just simply do a good job at being a cell and the rest will take care of itself.

Trust that it is in your best interest to form a symbiotic relationship with the greater body of Tao. You do your part to tend to the responsibilities Tao has assigned you, and it is in the Tao's best interest to care for all of your needs.

Wu-wei

The teachings of *wu-wei* are central to practicing the Tao. Wu-wei means "non-action" and "emptiness." The teachings of wu-wei stand in sharp contrast to our Western traditions of building a life through pursuing ambition. Wu-wei is to remain empty of ambition and open to the moment. The Tao and Te are the universal principles of Taoism, and wu-wei is the appropriate individual posture to take to best align with the natural order.

Non-action would be misinterpreted if taken literally. It does not mean not doing. It means not trying to impose yourself on life as if it is only your will and effort that is making it all happen. Instead of imposing your energy on life, you learn to enter into a relationship with the activity in front of you—you are taking part in the task getting done rather than doing it. This simple shift makes all the difference in the world. The trick is you can't will yourself to be with wu-wei. It is not something to achieve, instead you learn to drop into it. It comes from a natural arising born out of a knowing that you are a part of the same fabric of life that you see all around you. This leads to one of the key teachings on the Way of the Tao, the Path of Effortless Action.

> **The Path of Effortless Action:** ***Without doing anything, leave nothing undone.***

At first we puzzle over this enigmatic teaching and wonder, "If I don't do it, how is it going to get done?" It is a philosophical issue; where are you at within yourself while doing whatever it is you are doing? If you are mindful of wu-wei, instead of imposing your energy on the task in front of you, you would enter into a relationship with it, and it would be being done through you.

This emptiness is not self-denial; this would not be aligning with the power of the Way. It is staying open, not carrying an agenda, and staying present to receive from the moment. In this way, you respond to the task in front of you, knowing it has its own energy and need for completion, and if you are open, you get gently pulled into the activity. With wu-wei, you don't get exhausted at the end of the day. Tired after a hard day's work, yes, but not exhausted. You are not drawing on your private reserves of energy to apply to the task, instead you interact with the energy within the task and you take part in it getting done.

Of course this implies that you are responding to true needs. True needs carry their own Te and needs for completion, and when you merge with existing Te, your manifesting power is enhanced. If the dishes truly need to be done, instead of surrendering to doing them, surrender to them being done, and allow yourself to get pulled into the activity.

It is in a child's true nature that it has needs that it cannot meet by itself. If you surrender with wu-wei in response to these needs, the providing for these needs happens through you, not from you. The manifesting ability of your child's Te merges with your manifesting Te, and the right and perfect means for providing for your child's needs presents itself. This seems magical and naïve to a Western society that believes that results are just going to come from a lot of hard work. The trouble with this arduous path is that it becomes exhausting. How long can you carry that load?

Conversely, if a friend is putting pressure on you to do something that does not feel aligned with your true nature, you're just doing it because you think you should . . . this is not wu-wei. You have an agenda and will not be supported by the invisible Tao, and it will be exhausting.

A story helps illustrate this. When I met Laurie, my wife, I already had a son from a previous marriage. Since then, we have had three more sons, all now starting lives of their own. Family has been, and continues to be, the greatest gift that has come to me in this life. But I must admit to typical male resistance at each announcement of our growing family. "But we can barely afford our life as is." "Our house isn't big enough for another person." "We are just getting to a place where we can travel a bit, wouldn't another child restrict us?" Embarrassing now, but I have to admit these concerns. Laurie, great, unknowing Taoist sage that she was, always said, "Don't you know children come with their own resources? We'll get a bigger house and increased income when we need it."

Well, I didn't know this teaching back then, and I even must admit to a bit of chauvinistic judgment of "feminine nonsense," but I was willing to trust the depth of the conviction I saw in her. Now that our children are in various stages of leaving home and starting families of their own, I can reflect back on the truth of this teaching.

Although we didn't have the language for it back then, she was referring to the children's Te—the manifesting power of the Tao. That which can create the mountains and the oceans and all of nature, won't have much difficulty coming up with food and shoes for our children.

If it is in your true nature to have a family, your Te merges with the Te of your children, and your manifesting power is increased. You become a manifesting agent for the Te of your family. A way is provided if you surrender to the Tao and let it be revealed. This is not merely assuming the role of responsibility and being a provider, it is surrendering to the manifesting power of that role. Surrendering to power has nothing to do with sacrifice as in empty duty. It would always be in your best interest, and the best interest of everyone in your family, for you to surrender to this organizing and manifesting power of nature.

I adapted these teachings into a simple mental reminder that served me well in times of the worries, "Nature will support family life." I reasoned it was in nature's best interest that there be healthy families, and as long as I was willing to follow my true nature, nature would help provide the means for this to happen. Of course, I was blessed to be with a partner with whom it was also in her natural Te to raise a family. This is not always the case. Sometimes the basis of a loving relationship is not there, and then the Te would not be there to support a family and it becomes a struggle. For many, it is simply not in their Te to have children, and their Te leads them to pouring their creative, nurturing energy into other aspects of life.

Many are born in impoverished countries and in difficult times where the manifesting power of Te is going to be severely limited due to the scarcity of resources. It would be insensitive and even cruel to think that parents in these dire circumstances should be able to adequately provide for their children if they were in touch with their Te. Here, I would suggest that it is the natural Te of the global community to provide for our children. If we take the risk of doing what it takes to move global resources to troubled spots and feed the people, this would empower the global Te, and methods would be found to make it happen.

Emptiness

Wu-wei is also taught as emptiness. The door is useful because of what isn't there; the bowl is useful because of empty space within. Practicing emptiness means non-attachment; there is not only nothing to be held, there is also no one to be doing the holding. Picture space, the void within you. Staying empty, your behavior is not based on precedents, it remains fresh alive in the moment.

To be with the Tao, stay present to the moment by practicing emptiness—don't carry your agenda. If someone asks you if you would like a hamburger, and you answer, "No, thank you, I'm a vegetarian," you are not in the moment. How do you feel in the moment of the question? Make the decision fresh each and every time. Ask yourself. "Do I want a hamburger at this time?" Answer "no" if it is because you truly do not want it in this moment, not because of a rule. Maybe your answer will be "no" every time for the rest of your life; then you are being alive to the Tao of the moment rather than acting on a dead decision from a previous time.

A house is built with building materials, but it is that which isn't there, the empty space defined by the walls, that we actually use. Being and nonbeing co-exist together. It is the emptiness, the nonbeing that makes it useful. You have a form—a body and a life. That is the substance. When you are practicing emptiness within, you are not holding on to the form, nor making it happen with your will. It is happening, but not just of your will. Your life and its many involvements exist as the form, and when you are practicing wu-wei as emptiness, you are never carrying your life from one moment to the next—you begin to flow with it.

Yin-Yang and Mutual Arising

A core teaching of Taoism is the acceptance of polarity, yin-yang, and that both aspects of polarity mutually arise together and are inextricably bound to one another. That they exist together and essentially cause one another, and even dance with one another, is accepted as a given. Not a belief, as in something to have faith in, simple observation reveals polarity as part and parcel of the manifest world: male/female, dark/light, positive/negative; point of view, counterpoint of view, and so on. The ideal is to hold them in balance, knowing that they will constantly shift and even transform into each other.

This is most puzzling to the Western mind trained in the morality of good overcoming bad, of knowing the difference between right and wrong, and steeped in the belief that progress, progress, progress will lead to a better world. Hope reigns eternal.

There is no room for pursuing hope or indulging in fear in Taoism. It is neither fatalistic nor apprehensive. It is the great path of acceptance of the truth of the moment. "This is the situation I find myself in, so be it," would be the appropriate attitude. There is a gracefulness and fluidity to this philosophy that is far removed from the thrashing about of ambitious strivings.

Figure 9. YIN-YANG.

Like the famous yin-yang symbol, the white is the yang: masculine, strong, hard, dry, obvious, and so forth. The black is yin: feminine, receptive, moist, mysterious (ad infinitum). Each moves into the other and contains a dot of the other in its essence. The dark goes as far as it can go and then the seed of light within it begins to grow until it reaches its maximum, then the seed of dark grows again. This is why the Way of the Tao is not a moral path of right and wrong behavior. How one implies and creates the other is revealed in #2 of the Tao:

> Under heaven all can know beauty as beauty
> only because there is ugliness.
> All can know good as good only because there is evil.
>
> Therefore, having and not having arise together.
> Difficult and easy complement each other.
> Long and short contrast each other:
> High and low rest upon each other;
> Voice and sound harmonize each other;
> Front and back follow one another.
>
> Therefore the sage goes about doing nothing,
> teaching no-talking.
> The ten thousand things rise and fall without cease,
> Creating, yet not possessing,
> Working, yet not taking credit.
> Work is done, then forgotten.
> Therefore it lasts forever.[6]

Gentle and Yielding Power

The qualities of gentleness and maintaining a yielding attitude are encouraged throughout the teachings, but this is not any type of frailty whatsoever, this is the great strength and power of the Tao. The teachings tell us that a person is born gentle and soft, but when he dies he is hard; a young tree is flexible, but when it dies it becomes brittle, therefore gentle and yielding is the power of life.

As it reads in #76 of the Tao:

> A man is born gentle and weak.
> At his death he is hard and stiff.
> Green plants are tender and filed with sap.
> At their death they are withered and dry.
>
> Therefore the stiff and unbending is the disciple of death.
> The gentle and yielding is disciple of life.
>
> Thus the army without flexibility never wins a battle.
> A tree that is unbending is easily broken.
>
> The hard and strong will fall.
> The soft and weak will overcome.

We see this type of strength quite visibly when we watch someone practicing T'ai Chi. The postures and movements aren't harnessing the energy, instead, the energy seems to move the postures. The strength is evident in the graceful dancelike movements, not the strength that comes from flexing or resisting, no this is the fluid strength that responds to the moment and moves with the energy. Removing resistance, one learns to disappear from conflict.

Observe how a bird will swerve (most often) just before hitting a car responding with unseen eyes to the approaching danger. It is not there when the danger arrives. When you are in touch with the Tao, you also have this knack for avoiding conflict by not being there when it happens. It is not from backing down, it is from not being there in the first place. Your senses become so honed to energy of the moment that you sense conflict before it appears, literally. It is not avoiding issues, instead it is dealing with them before they become conflicts.

In a relationship, this gentle and yielding power would sense just before an issue was to move into dangerous territory, and deftly redirect the energy to avoid the conflict even before it appears. In family life with children, your antennae would perceive a shift in the children's energy just before trouble erupts. You might be involved with something else, but your energy field would sense the shift. Here again, you could skillfully redirect the children's energy even before the conflict presents itself.

The gentle and yielding power adds fluidity to your life; there begins to be a flow to your day.

The Three Gifts of the Tao

Sutra #67 tells us that the Tao has three treasures that we are advised to guard and keep: (1) love; (2) simplicity; and (3) daring not to be ahead of the world (patience).

The principles of love and simplicity we would expect from any spiritual teaching, but the third treasure of "daring not to be ahead of the world" deserves some consideration. To the Western view, being ahead of your time and on the leading edge of discovery is a good thing. The Taoist knows that being ahead of time, or behind, are both of the mind, not supported by the here-and-now, home of the Tao. There is no separating in Taoism, no ahead and behind—it is all part of the same Tao. To receive the gift we are encouraged to stay aligned with our times and be involved with the world as it is.

This teaching reveals that experiencing a connection to the Tao comes as deep love and compassion, not intellectual detachment. Simplicity is the way. And, by not daring to be ahead of your time, you stay present.

The Image of Li

Later Taoists expanded upon the traditional image of *Li* as the principle of something that distinguishes it from all others, and expanded its meaning to describe the cosmic order that interconnects all of reality into a vast web of mutual interdependence. Each part is as important as every other part in the grand scheme of Li.

In his book *Tao: The Watercourse Way,* Allan Watts described an image. "Just as every point on a sphere can be considered the exact center of the sphere, so every organ of the body and every being in the cosmos may be seen as its center and ruler."[8] Or said differently, everyone you meet is an actor in your movie, and you are an actor in their lives as well. Ah, Li.

The tree does its part and follows its Te. Li brings the water, the birds, and the bees. Tao animates it all. Trusting this feeling of living in harmony is the best and most you can do. This is typically plenty of work for most of us. Then you place your faith in the Tao. You do your part; Li takes care of how it all fits together with the rest of the world. This is beyond what the mind could do anyway, so one can rest the weary mind from trying to figure it all out. It can't be done. It is not your job. Tao takes care of that. If you were tending to your own path, the interconnectedness of all life would subtly alarm you, and, making adjustments to realign with harmony, would move you out of harms way if necessary.

Of course, this presupposes that you are honoring your feelings and living a harmonious life in the first place. If you are out of balance and you anticipate danger or an approaching problem, well, this is to be expected—it comes from the distorted lens you are looking through. However, if you are living with Tao and something feels amiss, pay attention to the subtle alarm and make an adjustment to restore harmony. And it is subtle; danger comes in pre-announced as a subtle prompting of something not feeling right. Again, if you are out of balance and not feeling right, and from this place sense something amiss, this is a reflection of your state of being and can't be trusted as the true voice of the Tao.

Remember, there are no rules.

It is not a game plan, nor a strategy; it's a moment-to-moment encounter with the Tao and Te that leads to safety. Then you can trust that fire cannot burn you, water cannot drown you, etc., because you wouldn't be there in the first place. It is living with assurance instead of insurance. This is far removed from our Western approach of insuring everything.

You don't have to do it all at once and cut off your current insurance polices and place all faith in Tao. Start where you are by honoring your feelings over your mind inch by inch, situation by situation, and start asking yourself, "What are my true feelings concerning the situation in front of me?" We are more often mental, overriding feelings with what makes sense, the plan, the strategy, and the goal.

The Tao and Death

The teachings from the Tao concerning death are unique among all the world's spiritual traditions in the apparent attitude of "no big deal." From the teachings on mutual arising, the statement "Being and nonbeing produce each other," shows how extensive the principle is. Because there is life, there is death. Because there is death, there arises life, following each other as day and night, as simple as that.

Chuang Tzu captures the attitude with this:

> Life and death are due to fate and their constant succession like day and night is due to Nature, beyond the interference of man. . . . The universe gives me my body so I may be carried, my life so I may toil, my old age so I may repose, and my death so I may rest.[9]

Like the teachings of the Buddha, Taoism does not go beyond what can be known. The universe gave me my body. This is a simple enough philosophy. I was given a body and that is that. No karma teachings. No original sin. Simply I am here. Not much planning for the afterlife, other than picturing it as rest. Now that we are here, alignment with nature is the way.

Chuang Tzu's words point us to staying present; be young when you are young, old when you are old, and dead when you are dead. The teaching also reminds us that death doesn't last all that long!

From the *Tao Te Ching*, Sutra #16 says it beautifully:

Empty your mind of all thoughts.
Let your heart be at peace.
Watch the turmoil of beings,
But contemplate their return.

Each separate being in the universe
Returns to the common source.
Returning to the source is serenity.

If you do not relate to the source,
You stumble in confusion and sorrow.
When you realize where you come from,
You naturally become tolerant,
Disinterested, amused,
Kindhearted as a grandmother,
Dignified as a king.
Immersed in the wonder of the Tao,
You can deal with whatever life brings you,
And when death comes, you are ready.[10]

Chuang Tzu writes:

> Having abolished the past and the present, he was then able to enter the realm of neither life nor death. Then to him the destruction of life did not mean death and production of life did not mean life. In dealing with things, he would not lean forward or backward to accommodate them.[11]

Chuang Tzu paints the picture that life and death follow each other continuously and are essentially one. Spending thought concerning distinctions between life and death pulls you out of the moment, thus is a distraction and irrelevant question. You are where you are; deal with it.

Applying the Teachings of the Tao in Everyday Life

Thus far we've explored the philosophical underpinnings of Taoism. The opportunities for applying these simple teachings into everyday life are endless. The following are some examples.

Harmony is the Measure

And how can one know if you are aligned with Tao, what is the gauge? "Take harmony as your measure," we are advised. If you are in harmony with yourself and life, trust this as the clue that you are on track. To live with the Tao, believe that the entire universe is acting within the laws of harmony within change. Tune yourself to harmony with all situations around you. Trust that harmony is the truth and conflict is the illusion. When you are in conflict within yourself, or with another, know that you are in illusion and don't trust any decisions you would make from this illusion. Wait until you come back to balance, then trust decisions you must make or actions to initiate.

A Need-to-Know Basis

Alan Watts used the delicious phrase "now-streaming" to describe the Way of the Tao. This staying absolutely present does not lend itself to accumulating knowledge. Instead of arming yourself with knowledge to prepare for potential situations, the Taoist path is to trust the information will be revealed when it is needed. You needn't shun learning, but engage the information while it is in front of you and then let go of it and trust it will be available on a "need to know basis."

The Tao of Inanimate Objects

Tao is extended to inanimate objects, and we all know things like cars, houses, and places have a feeling associated with them as well. The teachings from Feng Shui reveal the mystical art of placement and how various arrangements of a room create a totally different energy pattern and furthermore, how changing the energy flow of a particular environment can have an impact on all aspects of a person's life. The teachings of Feng Shui reveal that when a room is laid out with consideration for directions, colors, symbols, and the elements, the flow of chi can be enhanced.

Even without studying Feng Shui, you can cultivate this by paying attention to how you feel in each environment that you create for yourself such as your house, office, and bedroom. Do the feelings of the environment promote the intention of the room? Does the bedroom give a feeling of rest and comfort? If it is too busy, how will the psyche be at rest? If it is cluttered with tasks undone, this will make it difficult for the psyche to rest without a sense of guilt or neglected responsibility. So the simple rule is: Create the environment that supports the intent. Let all aspects of the room come into your consideration in that unifying perspective.

The Tao of Right Livelihood

Simplicity is a key throughout the teachings and we are advised to do our work, and then step back. We are encouraged to be mindful of our job while working and when done, walk away from it.

From #9:

> Chase after money and security
> And your heart will never unclench.
> Care about people's approval
> And you will be their prisoner.
>
> Do your work, then step back.
> The only road to serenity.[12]

Taoism promotes simplicity and quietness, but not a sheltered life. It would seem that Taoism would be best suited for a contemplative life in nature, but the *Tao Te Ching* also gives practical advice for worldly matters such as career, politics, and government. Although ambition is shunned, if it is one's true nature to be a leader, or manager, or person of authority, this also can be carried out in accord with the Tao.

Lao Tzu was writing at a time when the teachings of Confucius were dominant in China. Social responsibility as duty is a strong tenet of these Confucian teachings, and here, Lao Tzu stands in sharp contrast. With a strong belief in natural order, it follows that Lao Tzu would promote the renouncing of artificial roles, and that the government that interferes the least is the best, and the manager who remains inconspicuous in the work place is the most effective.

From #17:

When the Master governs, the people
are hardly aware that he exists.
Next best is a leader who is loved.
Next the one who is feared
The worst is the one who is despised.

If you don't trust the people,
You make them untrustworthy.

The Master doesn't talk, he acts.
When his work is done, the people say,
Amazing, we did it all by ourselves![13]

This sutra sets the Taoist standard for fulfilling a position of authority. Using the power of one's position to be effective in getting the job done, and no more. Instead of drawing attention, disperse the attention to the employees. Use your power to empower the workers.

Three in the Morning

There is a famous Taoist story from Chuang Tzu. An animal keeper was told to start rationing the portions of chestnuts given to the monkeys. When he told the monkeys that he would be giving them three measures in the morning and four in the afternoon, they loudly complained. So he said, "All right then, I'll give you four in the morning and three in the afternoon." This they agreed to.[14]

This simple story reveals so much of the spirit behind Taoism. Making the adjustment required no sacrifices for the animal trainer. Everyone gets their needs met and all is well. How often just a simple adjustment in our approach to a situation, based on the needs of the moment, would bring us back in touch with the Tao. When you insist that something has to be done one way and one way only, you are imposing your will rather than responding with wu-wei to the Tao. With wu-wei, you can fulfill your responsibility as a parent, teacher, employer, or animal trainer by responding and adapting to the needs of the situation, rather than imposing unbending will.

From Object to Field and Back Again

One of the key points to utilize to stay aligned with the Tao is the focus point of your attention. Learn to shift your attention from the object or issue in front of you to the larger field of everything going on that is influencing the current situation. You learn to see everything interconnected in a vast web. Then you return to the situation you are dealing with as a particular manifestation of the energy of the field, the Tao.

How this plays out in everyday life is to see a current event, say in a relationship, as part of a cycle. You learn to relax into the natural rhythms of your cycles of physical, emotional, and social life. As you come to know your most natural way of being, you honor these various cycles. For example, say you are a person who's natural emotional rhythm requires a few days of quality alone time for your well-being. If you proactively create this retreat time for yourself by conscious choice, this will not be a problem. If you forget, or don't know you need this down time and you try to push through it, well, we know what happens. The inevitable problem, frustration, or difficulty with someone, or something that forces you to get off all by yourself to work out the frustration. . . . In truth you needed to get off by yourself one way or another. So this is the field of your natural emotional cycle. The event is the current issue in your world; the object. As you learn to shift your focus from object to field to object again, it allows you to see how the details of your life fit within the big picture.

Another application is to shift your attention away from the current event, and redirect your attention to the energy behind the event. The energy is the field; the event is the object. See them both simultaneously. See the current event as an expression of the energy behind it. Question yourself, "Are there other ways I could be expressing this energy?" Is there some way that you can take that same energy and proactively engage it by expressing it consciously as choice?

Practicing Taoism leads to understanding energy. What is the energy behind desire? Desire is defined by not having. The "I Am" statement of energy is sent out as being separate from the object of desire. Desire pushes away. "I desire" translates as "I do not have". . . take a look at your energy statement and its result (how you feel). "I enjoy," now that is a different issue altogether. One of the simple and great teachings of the path can be expressed this way: If you want to experience more fulfillment in your life, learn how to spend more time wanting what you already have, and spend less time wanting what you don't have.

If you want to experience more fulfillment in your life, learn how to spend more time wanting what you already have, and spend less time wanting what you don't have.

For those on the "householder" path with family, relationships, career, and all the worldly responsibilities this path entails, the image of the Taoist sage walking along the streams of nature and at one with it all might seem like a welcome retreat, but not the normal day. Yes, it is ideal to be one with all of life, but not always realistic in family life, thus Taoism can seem like a remote ideal. Huston Smith says that it would not be unusual for a person to be Confucian in the householder years (a system much more aligned with responsibilities) and then retire into a life of Taoism. The question arises: Do you have to wait for retirement to practice Taoism? Going with the flow just doesn't cut it in the nine-to-five world, let alone with the moral responsibility involved with raising children.

This is the beauty of the Taoist path: no rules, no dogmas, and no right way to do it, only your way, the Way. There are principles in Taoism, not rules; you can apply these principles whatever your station is in life, particularly if you have stayed aligned with your true nature. If it is your true nature to raise a family, then you learn to be at one with it and go with the flow of family life.

Removing Judgments

As you practice being in the Tao; staying open, receiving, and practicing wu-wei is most readily accessible in raw nature where the life force is particularly strong. Much easier practicing deep acceptance with a tree than it is with family members! It is easy to walk though a stand of trees and accept each one as it is. The bent and gnarly trees are seen as just as beautiful as the tall, straight, perfect specimens.

We see this diversity of expression in nature and find it delightful. Wouldn't it be delightful to have this same acceptance for all the people in your life? This is removing the judgments that stand in the way of experiencing the Tao of the moment. Judgment immediately pulls you out of the Tao; you become frozen in your resistance. This doesn't mean not to have opinions or views, but learning how to be unthreatened by the view and opinions of others. You don't have to believe their view, just accept that it is their view and it does exist.

The Ongoing Story

A Taoist would never say, "So, that's how it turns out!" Life is always in a process of change and the Taoist would see how it is only in this moment. Like the famous story of the farmer whose horse ran away and the neighbor came over to commiserate his misfortune, but the farmer only replied, "Well, maybe." The next day, the horse returned accompanied by many wild horses, which followed it home. The neighbor came over to comment on the good fortune and the farmer replied, "Well, maybe." The next day the farmer's son broke his leg from attempting to ride one of the wild horses. The neighbor came over to comment on the misfortune, to which the farmer replied, "Well, maybe." The next day the army came by the village to enlist the young men, but not the farmer's son because of his broken leg. The neighbor came over to comment on the good fortune to which the farmer replied, "Well, maybe." The farmer knows life is an ongoing story.

Right Livelihood

Here's another story. Twenty years ago I owned and operated a restaurant with a few partners. I had a family with four sons and the restaurant was my livelihood and way of providing for my family. I was also a professional astrologer on the side. Astrology was my passion and true interest, but at that time, I didn't believe it could provide for my large family and their growing needs.

As my clientele kept growing, my life was becoming too crowded and, yet, I couldn't trust fully in the manifesting ability of the Tao. I had been using the *Tao Te Ching* as a guide for how to conduct myself with the restaurant and the commune we lived in. I was learning how to respond in a gracious way to the many pressures and responsibilities in my life, and yet I was becoming increasingly aware of the conflict within me. The Tao seemed to be pointing me toward astrology, and yet how could I trust the Tao to pay my bills?

We took the leap of faith, left the restaurant behind, moved to a remote area of the country that we were drawn to for raising our children and placed faith in the Tao. My doubting mind still had a back-up contingency plan in case this didn't work. I gave myself a year to get back to the same level of earning as with the restaurant and, if not, I'd go back to finding a job. Well, it took a month, not a year, to get to stable financial ground, and it has continued. There is no job security in being an astrologer, no sick leave, retirement benefits, nor guarantees that there will be work in next week's mail, yet the manifesting power of the Tao has continued to support our family. Cars and college educations and many things I don't consider particularly Taoist have come from surrendering to the Tao of parenting.

Manifesting with the Tao

Taoists are as famous for paradox as Zen is with its Koans. One of the paradoxes of Te is that you get it if you don't want it. To describe this, the universe will give back to you in like kind, a reflection of the energy you are putting out. If you are looking, you won't find because you are defining yourself as looking. If you are finding, you find more. If you affirm you are one with the Tao then, it will respond to your natural energy.

To apply this paradox would be to affirm energetically that which you want, as if you already have it. Send out the energetic message of being thankful and appreciative of having such and such and see what happens. Live energetically as if it was already true and see what happens. If you are sending out the energy of enjoying abundance, you attract it to you. If you send out the message of wanting wealth, you energetically are pushing it away by your own "I Am" statement.

Consulting the Tao

When you have a question or situation in front of you to consider, consult the Tao. To do this, first take responsibility for being aligned with the Tao. Make your decision from within the Tao by making sure you have first aligned with this to your own satisfaction. The Tao is most revealed through nature, so spending time in a favorite place in nature is the surest path to realign with the Tao. Watching the patterns water makes in a stream, leaves in their quivering dance with the breezes, or observing any natural movement in nature as if it were a tuning fork to bring you back into attunement.

Now, from within the Tao, return to your question. Take your entire feelings into account as you consider the question. When you decide upon a course of action, ask yourself, "Does this choice of action pull me out of the Tao, or am I able to maintain this felt connection to the deep harmony of the Tao?" You can feel if it is appropriate action for you by watching your feelings as you enter into your decision. You will feel if it is inappropriate for you if your decision pulls you out of your felt connection with the Tao.

The Garden Editor

I've learned to use my garden as an editor. When I'm in my study, I dream up all types of ideas and workshops. I've learned over the years that many of my ideas should have stayed in my office and were not connected to what would be meaningful for others. I've learned to go out in my garden and carry my ideas in my mind. I surrender to the gardening tasks of tending to nature and its needs. If, while I'm gardening, I'm able to hold on to my current idea while simultaneously tending to the needs of the garden, then I trust that this idea is fertile. If, however, I'm not able to simultaneously be one with the garden and hold on to my current ideas, I let them go and assume they are not fertile at this time.

This completes our exploration of philosophical Taoism and its applications in life. From here, Taoism branches into a complex web of beliefs and practices. After the philosophers like Lao Tzu and Chuang Tzu left the scene, Taoism began to merge with practically every other aspect of Chinese culture. Its very nature of being like water allowed it to absorb and assimilate almost every other school of thought as it swept across China. It is beyond the scope of this book to elaborate on all of the directions Taoism has taken, other than to comment on how vast it is indeed.

The stories told in *Chronicles of Tao,* by Deng Ming-Dao, reveal an era before Communist China when Taoist adepts would retreat to a sacred mountain far removed from the world. Here they would dedicate their lives to perfecting the various Taoist practices of meditation, martial arts, inner alchemy and Chi Kung, and longevity studies, including herbology, healing abilities, and the development of special powers. At the core of all these manifestations are the disciplines and practices of Taoism.

Discipline and Practices

Approaching life with an uncluttered mind is assumed in the teachings of the Tao. This is hardly a fair assumption for most of us! To get to an uncluttered mind will not simply happen in our Western culture. We are ambitious for education and accomplishments, and these grasping tendencies must be compensated for by some type of discipline in order to shift the focus, otherwise the ego-driven mind will have our constant attention. Without discipline, we would not be able to control the monkey mind, and the Tao could not be seen. We would be listening to our incessant and all-important mental chatter, and, consequently, missing the deeper currents of the Tao.

Tao without Te could lead to an indulgent, slovenly lifestyle supported by "just going with the flow." Experience shows that some discipline is necessary to pull out of the cultural neurosis at the mental level. Meditation training in not following the thoughts the mind generates is ideal. You cannot stop the thoughts from arising, but with practice, you can learn to not follow the thoughts. Practice is a good image, because the meditation practice is preparation for taming the runaway mind throughout the day when it is not practice, but the real thing. You learn to cultivate the observing part of your mind throughout the day. Stay in the observing mode: judgments, analyzing, memories, planning, and desires all tempt to grab your attention. Simply watch them as well.

Virtue is Te, the original pattern and the manifesting power that comes from being aligned with this pattern. This does not need to be created, it needs to be aligned with, and this is where discipline is required—not just simply giving into the ego's whims and calling it the Tao. Discipline raises your energy and is required for taming the wild mind syndrome. Aligning with Tao requires listening, dropping the comments, judgments, and preferences to simply receive one moment to the next.

Taoist Energy Practices and Chi

Philosophical Taoism seeks to align with the power of Te and conserve it, however, there are many disciplines that focus on increasing this power. The Taoist understanding of chi (also spelled *Ch'i,* or *qi,* and pronounced "chee") is the basis of all incredible skills that have been developed in Chi Kung, T'ai Chi, martial arts, Taoist healing practices, and Feng Shui. Acupuncture is a prime example of how specific the Taoists are in their understanding of how energy moves through the body.

Chi and the Tan T'iens

Chi is the subtle life force that animates life, and it rides on the wings of breath. Chi is breath, not just of air, but also of the universal life force. Chi accumulates and forms a reservoir of this vital energy in the lower abdomen, known as the *Lower Tan T'ien* (pronounced "don tien"). There are two other Tan T'iens; one in the region of the heart and the other near the brow, but it is this Lower Tan T'ien that is the main reservoir of chi, the vital life force, and when we say Tan T'ien without referencing which one, it is always the lower one we are speaking of.

The quality of your health and well-being corresponds directly to the quantity and movement of chi in the Tan T'ien. When the amount of chi is diminished by lifestyle choices, or becomes stagnant through lack of discipline, you become susceptible to illness. Conversely, with increased circulation of chi, your vital energy is enhanced, you feel better, have more energy, and your ability to manifest is dramatically improved. You simply operate at a higher level of energy. Your ability to handle stressful and challenging situations also improves, as your reserve's are not so easily depleted.

We all have a requisite amount of chi to maintain one's life. This chi can be enhanced in numerous ways, from traditional techniques of breathing, movement, and visualization exercises, to many a spontaneous magic moment that shifts the energy on its own accord. The magic moments are wonderful when they spontaneously shift you into a heightened state of awareness, like suddenly noticing sunlight sparkles dancing on shimmering water and feeling your energy shift. Shifting the energy is the important key. It is nice to know about the Tao, but it takes that heightened awareness to feel the aliveness of it. Spontaneous moments are the best. These natural peak moments of heightened awareness are treasures when they occur, but are all too rare. Thus the Taoists developed numerous techniques for cultivating a shift to a higher-level energy and awareness.

Heightened awareness is different from transcendence. Instead of withdrawing attention from the sensory world as in transcendent meditation, you become keenly aware of all senses and your interaction with the life force around you. From this state of awareness, you can interact and draw in chi through all of nature.

Nature Walk Exercise

On a walk in nature, where beauty is all around, let the experience resonate within you as if there were no separation between you and what you are seeing; feel the tree and let the tree feel you. This interchange refreshes and revitalizes your chi. Whatever you are seeing on your walk; experience it within you as well. Feel the leaves of your mind dance in a gentle breeze. Be one with the constant renewal within you as you watch a stream. Feel the stillness of mountain and the expansiveness of sky. Feel the tenacity of life within you when you see a tree growing out of a barren bank. Experience the birds in flight as winged thoughts passing through your mind. You are part of the same fabric that you are witnessing, and you merge with this in deep resonance. Let go of thoughts as they appear and stay present to experiencing the fullness of the moment with nature. Take appreciation one step further and know that the sensation you are experiencing is the actual flow of chi flowing between you and what you are appreciating.

On a walk in nature you can focus on drawing chi up from the earth with each step. And as you lift your foot up, feel the chi move through you and up into the heavens, drawing chi from the earth and sending it to the heavens with each step. Then reverse the image and picture yourself gathering energy from the heavens with your raised foot and sending the chi through you into the earth as you step down. Feel yourself as a conduit of energy moving both ways between the heavens and the Earth.

On your walk, enter into an energetic rapport with all you see; when you come to a tree, experience its ch'i and let it interact with yours. Watching the swirling patterns of a river, the graceful movement of leaves in the wind, light sparkling off water, any of these magic moments are opportunities to not just observe the phenomenon, but to take part in it. Feel the beauty you see in nature and let it awaken that same beauty in you.

It all starts from here. From mastery of martial arts, to Taoist healing imagery, to the basis of traditional Chinese medicine, to Taoist sexual practices, and many disciplines taking a lifetime to master. While what is done with this is many and varied, the core understanding of the circulation of chi and what one can do to enhance it is central to these arts. Instead of focusing one's attention on any specific point, Taoist energy practices are based on the movement and circulation of the chi, the light.

Chi is not adrenaline. It is energy, but not what we Westerners think of as high-powered, caffeine-induced drive. It is subtle energy. It might not look so subtle when we see a martial artist demonstrating incredible feats of harnessing and focusing this energy, but again, it is of a more subtle frequency than sheer muscle power. Since chi comes from the Tao, it is enhanced by a lifestyle in harmony with the Tao. Simplicity in all ways is the chief advice here, with very developed systems of health and hygiene practices to enhance the chi.

Exercise for Tan T'ien Breathing

Sit upright with your spine straight. The way of Tao is the way of water, thus let all your muscles be like water and sink to their lowest places. Now focus your attention on your abdomen, the region of your Lower Tan T'ien; not just a spot, the entire region just below your navel to your spine. This is the reservoir of your chi, the elixir of life, and should be honored as such. Now gently pull your breath down and into the Lower Tan T'ien. Feel your lower stomach all the way to your back expand with the breath. Breathe out by gently squeezing in at the Tan T'ien and up and out with the diaphragm. In, all the way down into the Tan T'ien, let it expand. Hold your breath for a moment, and then gently contract the muscles in this region on exhaling.

Use imagery and invite chi in on the wings of each breath. See it as a golden light and as you breathe into the Tan T'ien, see the chi accumulating and forming a pool of liquid light. As you continue, imagine the reservoir filling beyond full, and see the liquid light rising up and begin to fill the Middle Tan T'ien in your chest. As your heart fills to overflowing, the chi rises up as a golden light to the Upper Tan T'ien in your third eye. Imagine the chi continues to fill all three energy centers and still rises and spills over and begins to fill your entire body. Linger in this moment and feel the aliveness.

Chakras and Tan T'iens

The Tan T'ien system of understanding the flow of energy is closely aligned with the Chakra system from Hinduism. Prana is chi—same energy, different name. The Tan T'iens correspond to the Second, Fourth, and Sixth Chakras.

The chakras fall into three categories: the lower chakras (First, Second, and Third), the upper three (Fifth, Sixth, and Seventh) and where they meet in the Heart Chakra (Fourth). It can be seen from the figure that the Lower Tan T'ien is in a blending of the three of the lower chakras. The Middle Tan T'ien is right at the Fourth Chakra, and the Upper Tan T'ien is in the middle of the upper chakras, again, drawing from all three. Thus the Tan T'ien system corresponds to the three main regions of the chakras, and you can use your understanding of the chakras to aid in your understanding of the meaning of each of the Tan T'iens (see figure on page 149).

A key distinction between the chakras and the Tan T'iens is in how they image the energy. The Tan T'ien system views the energy as a field or reservoir, where the chakra system views the energy as a spinning vortex. Experiment with both. Which feels more natural to you?

Chi Kung and Inner Alchemy

Chi Kung (or Qi Gong) is the core discipline that is at the heart of all practices of "moving the energy." From the healing imagery work of inner alchemy, to physical exercises integrating movement, breath, and imagery to strengthen and rejuvenate one's chi, Chi Kung embraces a wide spectrum of disciplines and practices. T'ai Chi is born of this tradition, as are all martial arts. Both inner and outer disciplines focus the breath, the mind, and all of one's senses on awakening, aligning, and moving the chi.

Taoism has a long tradition of alchemy, both physical alchemy, which seeks to create the magical elixir of physical immortality, and inner alchemy, seeking the immortality of the soul. There are many fascinating legends of the immortals and those who have lived to hundreds of years of age. There are also the legends and tales of those who died experimenting with anything and everything in quest of the elixir of immortality. A wealth of information on the healing properties (and dangerous properties) of herbs has been a spinoff of this quest and Chinese medicine has been the recipient of this treasure.

Inner alchemy has become the dominant expression of this transformational science, perhaps because you don't run the risk of death if you do something wrong!

The techniques for circulating the light in its backward movement are discussed in *The Secret of the Golden Flower,* a Taoist

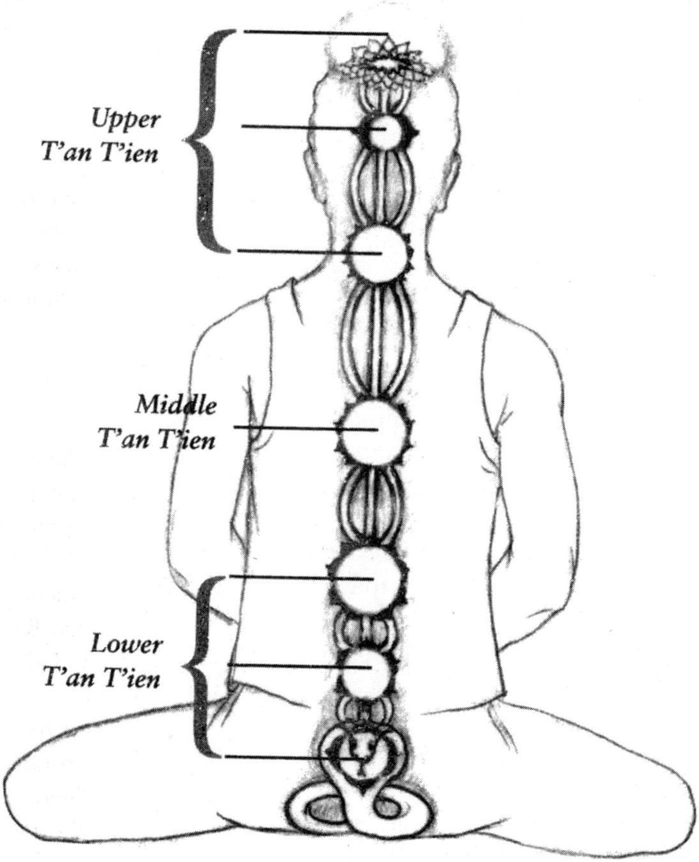

Figure 10. CHAKRAS AND T'AN T'IEN LOCATIONS.

classic for inner transformation. Translations have only recently surfaced in the West, although the teachings have been at the core of Taoist secrets for centuries. The golden flower is the Taoist name for what the Hindus call the thousand-petalled lotus. The principle is simple, but profound. For inner transformation to occur, circulate the chi inward, backward from its normal movement. The backward turning of the light is returning to the source, away from the senses. This is what the Hindus call *pratyahara:* "coming back home." The inner circulating of the light unites the male and female in an inner dance of energy and from this the Golden Flower blossoms.

The following are various practices from the inner alchemy tradition.

The Inner Smile

This beautiful and simple practice can be integrated easily into one's meditation practice. First close your eyes and imagine a friend approaching and feel a smile come over you. Pull the energy of the smile to your eyes and let this smile radiate through your eyes. The teachings then suggest directing the energy down specific meridians, but this can be simplified to gain the experience by visualizing the energy of this smile on a journey throughout your body. Just as you pulled the energy of the smile into your eyes, focus the energy of the smile on the inside of your head and brain; down your neck and throat—feel the inner smile at each place as it sinks into the body. Smile from your chest and lungs and let the smile settle into your heart. Enjoy a few breaths from the smiling heart and then take the smile through each of the organs: liver, kidney, pancreas, and spleen. Smile through each of your organs and then into your stomach, the intestines, the bladder, urinary tract, and colon. Smile from your sexual organs and then throughout the entire body through the blood network. Complete the meditation by feeling your entire body and being radiating the energy of the smile. Feel the healing radiance.

The Microcosmic Orbit

Two of the dominant energy channels of the subtle life force are readily identifiable: the Governing Channel and the Functioning Channel. The Governing Channel starts at the perineum (between the anus and the genitals), goes up the spine, over the top of the head, down through the brow, and ends at the roof of the mouth. The Functioning Channel runs from the tongue, down through the throat and neck, through the stomach, past the genitals, and ending at the perineum. When you place your tongue on the roof of your mouth, the circuit is complete. For ease of following the imagery, we will call the Functioning Channel the "Front Channel" and the Governing Channel the "Back Channel."

The practice of the Microcosmic Orbit uses breath and imagery to move chi through the circuit. First, sit in a comfortable meditation posture with your spine straight. Place your tongue on the roof of your mouth to connect the circuit and start the practice. On the in-breath, pull chi up through the Back Channel, up from the perineum, through the spine, over the top of your head, through your brow, and to the roof of your mouth. On the out-breath, feel the chi move down your tongue and throat, through your chest and stomach, through your genitals to the perineum.

Use imagery and trace the movement of chi with your mind's eye. You can use a ball of light, a wave of energy, a comet, or whatever works for you. In-breath, up the back. Out-breath, down the front. Feel this as cleansing and energizing your entire energy field. After several cycles, reverse the process and breathe up through the Front Channel and out through the Back Channel. Again picture the moving chi as both cleansing and revitalizing your entire energy field. Feel the yin-yang dance of your energy—the female/male, the receptive/assertive—feel these polarities blending and shifting into one another on the changing of the breath.

You can do this practice as long as you like. If you get dizzy or lightheaded, you are advised to stop the practice and work on grounding yourself before you begin again. The practice serves as a general tonic to your energy field. Without discipline, the imagination leaks vital chi in its wanderings; with a practice like the Microcosmic Orbit, the imagination is trained to serve you in a revitalizing way.

I often recommend this practice to people who feel their life is spinning out of control. In astrology, this is often the case with Uranus transits, where the energy quickens, uncertainty is everywhere, and a sense of major impending change is imminent. Even if you don't know your current astrology, you do know when you feel particularly anxious, like a cat on a hot tin roof, or like you

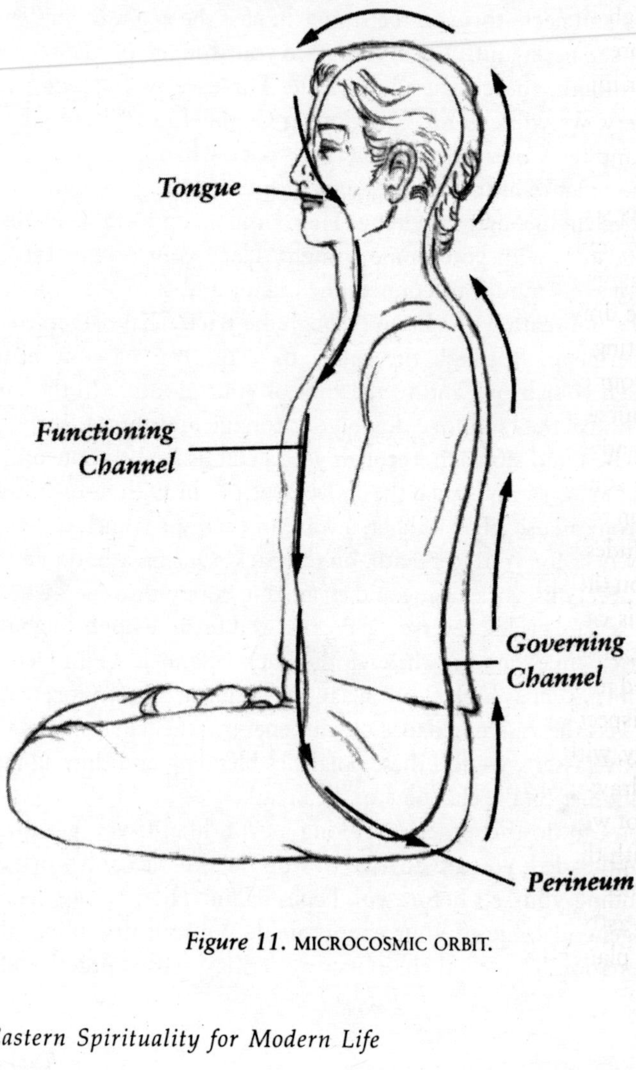

Figure 11. MICROCOSMIC ORBIT.

want to jump out of your skin. This is when you will find the greatest value in practicing the Microcosmic Orbit.

In these high-anxiety times, there is simply too much energy coursing through your body to be contained in your everyday life. By creating a circuit for the chi to move through your entire body, including the upper energy centers, you liberate the energy from personality issues. This frees you to express the energy in regions of the higher mind and creativity. When transformed through this practice of inner alchemy, the same energy, which was previously overwhelming, becomes the creative fuel of the higher mind.

Drawing Energy from Celestial Bodies

Taoists see the whole universe as interconnected in a vast web of energy, and thus even the sun, moon, planets, and stars are considered as vital sources of energy. Their light carries energy and this can be drawn into oneself to supplement one's own vital reserves. Squinting at the sun so that you see individual rays of light coming into your eyes is a great technique for drawing energy from the sun. Of course, natural caution of not looking directly into the bright sun is advised, but at sunrise and sunset particularly, it is quite safe if one squints and just lets in these individual rays. Feel your connection to the solar life force as if the scope of your being is so vast, it includes the sun and beyond. Picture vital chi entering into your eyes on the rays of light.

This can also be practiced with the moon, planets, and stars. You can stare directly into the moonlight and feel yourself being bathed in its cool light. Moonlight rejuvenates the feminine, receptive aspect of your energy. With the sun, you draw in powerful energy, with the moon you draw in soothing, nurturing energy. As you draw in the energy of the moon, let it cleanse your emotional field of worries and concerns. Feel its light as an emotional tonic.

With the planets and stars we can draw in universal wisdom. It is nice to know which planet is which and this can be found in most astrological calendars. When you are fortunate enough to see a planet and know which one it is, you can draw from that planet's energy. Here we can use the understanding of the planets from astrology to complement the Taoist visualization practices.

Mercury: Mercury never travels far from the sun and will only be seen near sunrise or sunset. Gather Mercury's light to empower your mental energy. Mercury rules all things of the mind; learning, thinking, talking communicating, etc., and drawing in Mercury's light improves mental capacity in all ways.

Venus: Venus is also a close companion to the sun and will only be seen near sunrise and sunset. Venus is the goddess of love and the patron of the arts. Her light enhances the aesthetic side of your character and gives you a greater ability to appreciate the beauty in all things. Her energy also stirs your romantic nature.

Mars: Mars is the warrior and looking into its reddish light empowers you with courage, strength, and the ability to assert yourself. Not the best choice if you are already agitated; its energy escalates hostilities, but if you need to make a stand, or if you need courage to start a new endeavor, Mars is the one.

Jupiter: Jupiter is the largest of planets and inspires confidence, optimism, and the ability to frame things in a positive light. Draw in Jupiter's light when you need to see the bigger picture. If you are getting ready for a journey, or simply want to travel and move out beyond existing boundaries, or want to draw a little luck into your life, Jupiter can help.

Saturn: Saturn is the taskmaster and when you need to draw in the strength to be more disciplined, Saturn's light is the best. Saturn's energy is ideal when you need to get organized, focused on a task, or need the perseverance to complete a project. Saturn demands self-mastery, so only draw on Saturn if you are willing to embrace the self-discipline it demands.

We have been describing the process of actually seeing the physical planet and drawing energy in this way. However, when you are not so blessed to be with clear skies, or the planet of choice is not in a visible place in the heavens, this same energy can be activated with visualization in meditation. Invoke a connection to the planet that embodies the teachings you need. First visualize the planet in the heavens and gradually merge with the planet until you are it, and it is you; you know what it knows and it knows what you know. Picture yourself absorbing the knowledge of the planet into your being, different than thinking about it; become it.

The Outer Practices of Chi Kung

The outer practices combine physical movement with the breath and visualization exercises of inner alchemy. Rigorous training is required and the body becomes a fine-tuned expression of the movement of chi. All of the martial arts have been born from this tradition as well as T'ai Chi. One needs proper teachers and training to pursue these practices, thus their methodology is far beyond the scope of this book. However, we will explore T'ai Chi as an example of integrating the teachings into daily life.

T'ai Chi

T'ai Chi is a martial art that embodies the teaching of Tao. Some would question if it actually is a martial art because it is not combative, but there is no question as to whether it is a discipline for self-defense on the one hand, and promotes health and well-being on the other. Primarily it is a practice for aligning with the Tao and restoring one's natural Te. It is in the nature of the Tao to support all life, but when your lifestyle doesn't support your natural Te, it no longer can function as a safety net. The series of movements of the T'ai Chi practice distributes the chi to all of the vital energy centers, revitalizing one's Te.

The characteristic gentle and dancelike movements of T'ai Chi are unmistakable. Each of the postures within the dance are indeed martial art postures, but in T'ai Chi the strength is being expressed inwardly, and not in strong body movements. The body remains supple and fluid from one posture to the next, like the flow of the Tao. All movement is initiated from one's center, the Lower Tan T'ien, thus, at each moment throughout the routine, there is balance. The T'ai Chi practitioner develops a refined sensitivity to the subtle currents of chi, not just in practice, but also in all of life.

T'ai Chi is yoga in movement. With Hatha Yoga, there is stillness in the postures; in T'ai Chi, the stillness is within, but there is constant movement in the outer practice. There is a constant balancing of yin and yang postures; for every forward movement, a backward movement; for every upward movement, a downward movement; never fully extending, never fully retreating, never reaching one's limit. Breath and mind integrated with each posture, T'ai Chi integrates the principle of harmony within change into the body.

Yielding is the way to strength in T'ai Chi as with the Tao. But this is not backing down in every conflict. It is a graceful movement in response to approaching energy, away from resistance and confrontation, becoming empty to approaching conflict, retreating to a position of strength and balance. The T'ai Chi practitioner uses the energy of the opponent, and, like the Tao, conserves energy by not resisting.

When applied as a philosophy for daily living, this translates as disappearing from conflict throughout the day. The Tao seeks lowly places and goes around obstacles. Thus, in the T'ai Chi of daily living, there is nothing to defend. You absolutely remove yourself from defensiveness and resistance to the moment, and when conflict approaches, you sense it ahead of time and move accordingly to go around the obstacle, always moving from your center.

As in the example of the bird that swerves at the last moment to avoid collision, responding with unseeing eyes to move out of harm's way, this is the T'ai Chi of daily living. You sense when adjustments are necessary to avoid collisions with others and remove yourself from harm's way just at the last moment. But no time to reflect on these glories, the next moment is already presenting itself, and gone, if you are not present with it.

In T'ai Chi, peacefulness is the way, yes, but not mere acquiescence, instead true adaptation to the needs of the moment, nothing to resist. Knowing that for every yin there is a yang and they always change into one another, you choose not to hold rigid opinions, and thus, nothing to defend. When opposition presents itself, you become empty. When life presents itself, you embrace. Without resistances, and initiating all activities from your center, your life becomes fluid in all ways.

Taoist Sexual Practices

The Taoist teachings of the role of sexuality in maintaining health and contributing to longevity are unique in all the world's spiritual traditions. Gone are the trappings of morality, guilt, and shame so common in spiritual teachings concerning sexuality. Gone also is some of the romanticism. Sexuality is considered the strongest force in nature and the deepest well of chi; obviously Taoists seeking to increase chi are not going to ignore this source. One is encouraged to draw from the well, and yet, not to spill out and waste the vital life force. Semen in particular, but all sexual fluids in general, are considered to be the life-giving nectar. Thus the teachings point to retaining these fluids and circulating them within.

The famed Yellow Emperor, who is credited as bringing forth the teachings of the five-element tradition of Taoist healing techniques, is also credited with putting forth the teachings of Taoist sexual practices. Legend has it that he maintained a harem of 1,200 women as lovers, and although he maintained sexual relations with all of them regularly, he never once ejaculated and lived to be hundreds of years old. Thus the teachings of Taoist sexual practices were born 5,000 years ago.

The Yellow Emperor had teachers as well. Legend has it the three sisters, the Plain Girl, the Mysterious Girl, and the Rainbow Girl, taught him the secrets of awakening the life force energy of sex through practices that are healing, rejuvenating, and hold the promise of leading to immortality.

The main teaching is of the vital importance of awakening sexual energy, yet maintaining your sexual fluids. There is no question of sexual superiority in Taoism; women are superior. From the Sutra #43: "The softest thing in the universe overcomes the hardest thing." Women naturally retain the sexual fluids from love's embrace, while the man loses this vital essence through ejaculation. It might seem like the teachings are mostly male specific, and this is because women don't have the problem of retention of the sexual fluid—it naturally happens. It was women, after all, who revealed the sexual secrets to the Yellow Emperor!

Semen retention is not as important for young men before the age of thirty-five; the body is still a veritable semen factory. The body diminishes in its ability to regenerate semen after thirty-five and it becomes more valuable to know the practices. Sexual activity is still strongly encouraged to awaken the life elixir, but particularly after fifty, it becomes important not to ejaculate as often to retain the vital life force. Even for young men, practicing periodic semen retention combined with the visualization exercises leads to increased vitality and clarity in all areas of life.

The pleasure associated with physical orgasm and ejaculation can be transmuted so that the orgasm is experienced without ejaculating. This is done by reversing the flow of semen.

Reversal of the Flow

Although retention of the semen is the high road, celibacy is not the ideal. The sexual energy is not to be avoided—that would miss out on this tremendous energy source. The basis of the teaching is reversal of the flow. For a man this means semen retention overtly, but also calls for a reversal of one's attention. Instead of the rush to orgasm and the release of energy being the focus of attention, one learns to recycle the energy with attention. Instead of a goal-oriented approach with the climax being the peak of the mountain, enter into the valley of lovemaking and let your energy meander through this field.

As an alternative to picturing the semen discharging, picture it being redirected upward. There are techniques, including pressure points, described in detail in books mentioned in the suggested reading list, but for starters, just slowing down the male ejaculation has benefit for both partners. The male, yang energy, rises to the occasion quickly, yet tires just as quickly after it expends itself. The female, yin, responds slowly to arousal, but can sustain much longer than the male—a common frustration in many a relationship. At minimum, the Taoist practices of slowing down the male ejaculation can help bring greater harmony to the pace of arousal within relationships.

Yin-Yang of Sexuality

Nowhere is the energetic dance of yin and yang so evident as in sexuality—the chi gets cooking in the dynamic interchange. By internalizing this yin-yang dance, you can greatly enhance the experience itself and rejuvenate your supply of chi like nothing else can. The man can embrace the yin in his partner to such a degree that he merges with the feminine within. The woman can receive the yang force to the degree it awakens this same male energy within. This implies heterosexual relationships, but the same principle would apply in same-sex relationships, the same yin-yang dance is not gender specific.

This requires a tremendous amount of mindfulness and takes some of the sheen off romantic images of love. Instead of getting lost in the romantic feelings toward your partner, you are encouraged to stay mindful of your own energy, and by reversing the flow, you don't send out all of your energy to your lover, you pull it up and inwardly.

Literally pull the awakened energy up your spine. You can use your eyes by picturing them energetically connected to the genitals, and, as you roll them upward in their sockets, feel them pull the energy from the genitals upward. You can use the muscles that you would use to stop yourself in the middle of peeing to squeeze off the outward movement of your sexual energy and send it upward. You can picture yourself making love with all aspects of your lover: the physical, emotional, mental, and spiritual. There are numerous techniques and visualizations to divert attention from the genitals to higher energy centers. The following is an example.

The Microcosmic Orbit for Two

The Microcosmic Orbit exercise described earlier in this section is an excellent method for pulling the energy from the sexual organs and circulating the energy through your entire being. When practiced with a partner, and both people are visualizing the energy moving through their interconnected energy fields, this greatly facilitates a merging at all levels.

First, both individuals should practice the Microcosmic Orbit within themselves while making love in the basic Tantric Sexual posture of the man sitting upright and the woman sitting on his lap, face to face (Figure 12). Once you are both successful at moving the chi through your entire system, you can proceed to the Microcosmic Orbit for two. Touch your tongues together to complete the circuit; you are already connected at the genitals. Visualize the energy moving up your Front Channel, up from the genitals, through your internal organs, up through the heart and chest, up the throat and to the tip of your tongue. Now see the chi move to your partner's tongue, up through the brow and crown, down the back of the head and spine to the perineum (shown as points in Figures 12–15), and then up your partner's Front Channel, connecting again with your tongue. As you receive the energy through your partner's tongue, visualize it moving up through your brow and crown of your head, down your backside, to the perineum. Then up your front side to repeat (Figure 13, see page 162).

An alternative route to experiment with would be to picture the exchange of energy at the genitals. Picture drawing chi from your partner through your connection at the genitals; pull this energy up your spine and over the top of your head to the roof of your mouth. Then picture it moving down your Front Side Channel, connecting with your partner's genitals. Follow your chi as it moves up the Front Channel of your partner, over the top of the head and down the spine to connect with you at your genitals (Figure 14, see page 162). Repeat and reverse the flow.

Of course, there are many ways to experiment with the yin-yang polarities in the Microcosmic Orbit for two. Be creative. Imagine both of your Front Channels as one. Picture the energy created in the genitals as rising up this combined

Figure 12. MICROCOSMIC ORBIT FOR TWO (BEGINNING POSTURE).

Figure 13. MICROCOSMIC ORBIT FOR TWO (RECEIVING ENERGY).

Figure 14. MICROCOSMIC ORBIT FOR TWO (CONNECTING ENERGY).

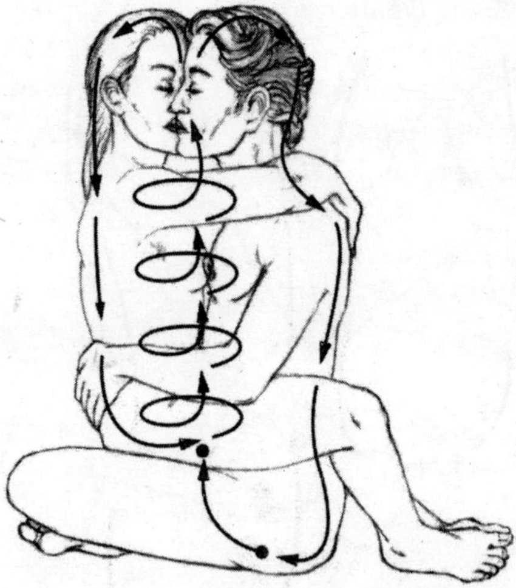

Figure 15. MICROCOSMIC ORBIT FOR TWO (MERGING ENERGY).

energy channel and when it reaches your tongues, take it to your individual third-eye, to your crown, and let the energy shower down your spine—to merge with your partner's energy once again to start another fountain of energy (Figure 15, previous page). Be creative. Use your imagination.

Obviously, in this short section on Taoist sexual practices, we've only touched on that which volumes are written about. Still, this presents an understanding of the general attitude and techniques of these practices. For many, this might be all the information you need to incorporate the Taoist understanding of sexuality into your own lovemaking. For others, this might only whet your appetite for more information and practices, and there are books listed in the Suggested Reading for that purpose.

If you already are in a relationship with an established personal style of your lovemaking, it is not easy to simply abandon your previous style and shift to the Taoist techniques. Expect a bit of this; ingrained sexual patterns have a strong pull, and we have not been raised on Taoist sexual practices. For many, I think it is best to adapt the Taoist understanding into your natural style and incorporate what is helpful without disrupting the flow of energy. Too much technique and not enough romance can be a real killer of the energy.

For romantics: Yes, it is possible to enjoy the romantic feelings and breathe them through the body as well. It's not about denying any of your natural sexual appetite, it's about cultivating this, and more, by bringing one's full self into lovemaking and being aware of the exchange of energy taking place at all levels.

Conclusion to Taoist Energy Practices

While reading the *Tao Te Ching,* it is relatively easy to feel the peace of the teachings, but then we don't always feel peaceful in our lives. This is when the practices are useful—they get the energy moving. Obviously, the practices of Taoism are many and varied, which allows for different temperaments. If your energy is blocked, or particularly if your emotional energy is entangled and ensnarled with another, do the practices to regain your center and call your energy back within yourself. When you are feeling anxious and nervous, turn to a practice of your choice. By moving the chi through one technique or another, you become grounded and able to sustain the higher frequency of energy and express it as creative choice.

Engaging the practices when you are already centered strengthens your spiritual resolve. The discipline of self-control that it takes for the practices is what it takes to consciously shift the energy and manifest from our clearest Te.

After Thoughts

The Tao is eternally present in the spontaneous moment. You don't picture Taoist priests getting together and reminiscing old times or planning future reunions.

—David Pond

Tai Chi while juggling: a metaphor for the Western Taoist.

—David Pond

"Small knowledge cannot understand big knowledge. Those with little experience cannot comprehend those with great experience."[15]

—Chuang Tzu (300 B.C.E.)

The *Tao Te Ching* ranks right behind the Bible as being translated into more languages than any other book in the world.

—David Pond

Being in an argument about the Tao is an oxymoron. . . .

—David Pond

Worry, fear, grasping, and doubt, these are the enemies of the Tao.

—David Pond

Taoism is a great antidote for the hurry, hurry, chase, chase lifestyle—it gets you present.

—David Pond

Nature knows the way to be nature. It is in its nature to do so. We are part of nature and by aligning with it as a teacher it can show us how to become human. By following your true nature your true nature is revealed.

—David Pond

Taoists would cringe at the modern world's efforts to bring nature under control. They would believe that we were destroying that which we were meant to revere.

—David Pond

Suggested Reading

Chan, Wing-Tsit. *A Sourcebook in Chinese Philosophy.* Princeton, N.J.: Princeton University Press, 1963.

Cleary, Thomas. *The Essential Tao.* New York, N.Y.: HarperCollins Publishers, 1991.

———. *The Secret of the Golden Flower.* New York, N.Y.: HarperSanFrancisco, 1991.

Feng, Gia-Fu and Jane English. *Tao Te Ching.* New York, N.Y.: Vintage Books, 1972.

Ming-Dao, Deng. *Everyday Tao.* New York, N.Y.: HarperSanFrancisco, 1996.

———. *The Chronicles of Tao.* New York, N.Y.: Harper Collins, 1993.

Mitchell, Stephen. *Tao Te Ching.* New York, N.Y.: Harper & Row, 1988.

Ni, Hua-Ching. *Tao: The Subtle Universal Law.* Santa Monica, Calif.: Seventstar Communications. 1979.

———. *Entering the Tao*. Boston & London: Shambhala, 1997.

Palmer, Martin. *Taoism*. Boston, Mass.: Element Books, 1991.

Reid, Daniel P. *The Tao of Health, Sex, and Longevity.* New York, N.Y.: Simon and Schuster (Fireside), 1989.

Watts, Alan. *Tao: The Watercourse Way.* New York, N.Y.: Pantheon Books, 1975.

Wong, Eva. *Cultivating Stillness.* Boston, Mass.: Shambhala, 1992.

Yudelove, Eric Steven. *The Tao & The Tree of Life.* St. Paul, Minn.: Llewellyn Publications, 1999.

———. *Taoist Yoga and Sexual Energy.* St. Paul, Minn.: Llewellyn Publications, 2000.

Endnotes

1. Mitchell, Stephen. *Tao Te Ching.* p. 56.
2. Chan, Wing-Tsit. *A Sourcebook in Chinese Philosophy.* p. 53.
3. Ibid. pp. 163–164.
4. Mitchell, Stephen. *Tao Te Ching.* p. 5.
5. Watson, Burton (trans.). *The Complete Chuang-Tzu.* p. 182.
6. Feng, Gia-Fu and Jane English. *Tao Te Ching.* p. 2.
7. Mitchell, Stephen. *The Tao Te Ching.* p. 76.
8. Watts, Alan. *Tao: The Watercourse Way.* p. 53.
9. Chan, Wing-Tsit. *A Sourcebook in Chinese Philosophy.* pp. 193–194.
10. Mitchell, Stephen. *Tao Te Ching.* p. 16.

11. Chan, Wing-Tsit. *A Sourcebook in Chinese Philosophy.* p. 196.
12. Mitchell, Stephen. *Tao Te Ching.* p. 9.
13. Ibid. p. 17.
14. Merton, Thomas. *The Way of Chuang-Tzu.* p. 44.
15. Cleary, Thomas. *The Essential Tao.* p. 64.

TANTRA

THE SPIRITUAL PATH in most great traditions that recognize a deity involves renouncing the worldly and physical aspects of life in favor of inner rapport with the Divine. Being born itself is taught as a separation from God as in the fall from Divine Grace. The sensory world is typically looked at as a distraction to the spiritual path by some, and the chief obstacle to the path by many. Here is the revolution of Tantra; it breaks from the Vedic tradition of renouncing the material world, and views the material world, not as an illusion veiling God, but instead, an expression and extension of God. God is beyond the material world, but every aspect of the material world, and our existence, is infused with God and no other. God and creation are one. To deny creation is to deny God.

It is taught that the teachings of Tantra were given because of the specific nature of the age we are in. In the Hindu system of time, most authorities affirm that we are deeply embedded in the Kali Yuga, a Dark Age.[1] The Kali Age started approximately 3,102 B.C.E. and is said to last for a total of 432,000 years. (See the Hinduism section on "Cycles of Time," page 77.) The Tantra teachings are said to be particularly well suited for this age, where sensuality and materialism have their strongest pull. In the Kali era, the mass of humanity is far removed from a peaceful and spiritual life. This is an age of strong desires for materialism and sensationalism, in contrast to more contemplative lifestyles in spiritual ages.

Tantra embraces all of life as Divine. Where other religions teach the oneness of God, this is most often taught as a transcendent oneness. Even Advaita Vedanta, the nondual path in Hinduism, teaches this oneness as existing on a separate order, not continuous with ordinary states of consciousness. One of the definitions of Tantra is "continuum"; the Divine expressed on all levels, including the material world and the body. Tantra practice leads to a truly unitive state of consciousness.

Both Hinduism and Tibetan Buddhism have a Tantra tradition. Although somewhat different in their orientation, both share the teaching that pleasure of the senses is not an obstacle to the spiritual path and can be used as a type of fuel to further one's spiritual progress. A Western Tantra is emerging of its own, which has a decidedly sexual flavor. We will explore this, but first let's explore its roots, as it is a growing hybrid of the two older traditions.

Hindu Tantra

From Hinduism, the Tantra teachings were first revealed as dialogues between Shiva and Paravati, the feminine goddess who could be personified by any of the feminine deities such as Uma, Kali, Durga, Lakshmi, Saraswati, and most particularly, Shakti. These dialogues reveal the techniques for awakening to the Divine feminine energy.

The Goddess Shakti

Shakti is the goddess of choice for those on the Tantra path. Shakti is the feminine expression of the latent energy of Shiva. Shiva is one of the three manifest expressions of Brahman, Brahman being beyond form and description (see Hinduism section, pages 53–56). Shiva is archetypal, still, quiet, inert. In the dance of Shiva and Shakti, it is the energy of the goddess Shakti that is courted. Shakti is the goddess that brings the archetypal Shiva to life. It is Shakti's erotic dance with Shiva that brings the world to life, revealing the essential erotic nature of creation. Shakti is the passion for the Divine. In the human realm, she awakens the kundalini and causes it to rise in the sushumna channel to awaken the upper chakras of Divine awareness.

Shakti: *It is Shakti's erotic dance with Shiva that brings the world to life, revealing the essential erotic nature of creation.*

Shakti energy can come from many sources. When a guru practices shaktipat with a disciple, a touch to the forehead or spine from the guru can send the awakened Shakti through all of the chakras and the disciple experiences sudden illumination. These shaktipat charges are not sustainable, but for a time, the disciple can experience awakened energy like never before. Anything that carries tremendous energy is loaded with Shakti.

There are three main Tantra paths in the Hindu tradition: the left-hand path, the right-hand path, and the integrated path (Kaula). The left-hand path is accused of debauchery by those of the right-hand path because of its open acceptance of sexual and other means of pleasure as available paths of experiencing the Divine. Those on the right-hand path practice rigorous purification practices including fasting, postures, and meditation as the means to awaken the energy. The left-hand path is fraught with dangers of addiction to the sensory world of pleasures in the name of spirituality. Still, the Tantric philosophy is that the sensory world can be a tremendous resource of prana, the vital life force that can be woven together with the awakened higher consciousness. The integrated path uses any and all sources for awakening to higher consciousness.

We will explore Tantra as a philosophy for living life and leave the specific mantras, postures, mudras, and yantras associated with Tantra for the books that focus on this track. Tantra is life-embracing as opposed to life-negating. India has always had a strong tradition of renouncing the body and its senses as an illusion and, basically, a karma-making factory. Tantra does not renounce the body. Tantra is life-affirming and thus looks at the body as part of God's expression, a vessel for the Divine.

Tibetan Buddhism Tantra (Vajrayana)

The teachings of the Buddha fall into two schools: Sutra and Tantra. The Sutras encapsulate the teachings; the Tantras, the techniques of actualizing the teachings. Sutra is the path covered in the Buddhism chapter, and focuses on the slow, steady path of awakening. Tantra is also attributed to the Buddha and is the fast track to awakening. Legend has it that a king was interested in the teachings of the Buddha, but he had his kingdom to rule and could not leave it to join Buddha's Sangha. He asked the Buddha if there were teachings for him to attain spiritual enlightenment, and the Buddha offered the teachings of Tantra. The intent of Tantra is to transform all worldly pleasure into spiritual bliss, thus one needn't renounce the world.

In the Buddhist tradition, Tantra refers to various texts such as medical Tantras or astrological Tantras that teach a system of techniques for actualizing higher states of consciousness. The main thrust of Buddhist Tantra is visualization, particularly of the deity you are working with. The technique is to visualize the deity of choice, typically a Buddha, but you could use Jesus or a special teacher for you. You visualize the being in complete detail from head to toe, including clothes, body and hand postures, facial expression, and the look in the eyes. The point is to concentrate so fully on the deity that you become the deity.

There are books in the suggested reading section that illuminate this process in great detail, but for our purpose we can summarize the Tibetan Tantra teachings as groundwork for Western Tantra.

The Resultant Path

Tibetan Tantra takes the future result of full spiritual awakening as the starting point, thus it is called "the resultant path." You begin as if you are already there! All guilt, shame, and self-debasement are looked at as a spiritual perversion. "You are a Divine being experiencing a human life," would be the proper attitude. The Sutra path works on attaining Buddhahood, while the Tantra path begins with this at the premise. I once heard the saying "If you pretend to be something long enough, you eventually become what you were once pretending." You begin by viewing yourself and others as Divine beings.

Searching for Pleasure

Pleasure is not looked down upon. However, this does not come from what we typically think of as bringing us pleasure. "There's nothing wrong with pleasure," teaches the Buddha; it is the grasping for objects and experiences that we *think* will bring us pleasure that creates ultimate disappointment. It is the searching for pleasure as if it were something outside of ourselves that is illusionary. Why search for pleasure when your very nature is bliss?

Yogic practices of redirecting the energy that normally runs through the nadis (see Hinduism section) and bringing it to the central channel (the sushumna) is the technique for transforming ordinary sensory experiences into cosmic bliss.

Renunciation

Since all worldly experiences are temporary, the first step is renunciation. This is not renouncing the world as in the ascetic path. This is renouncing attachment to the objects of the material world as if they were the source of pleasure. This is the practice of cultivating detachment instead of attachment. You still enjoy the pleasures of the material and sensory world, but knowing that they come and go, you stay detached.

Bodhichitta

The second step is Bodhichitta, awakening the heart. Buddhist practices are based in compassion and you awaken your heart so that you might help all beings to be more loving and accepting of life. Vipassana meditation can help to quiet the mind. Breathing in the qualities of love and joy can help. Inviting your guru or special teacher into your heart can help. But one way or another you rest in your Awakened Heart.

Meditating on the Bardo States

Bardos were discussed in the Buddhism chapter as the transition states after death and before the next rebirth. In Buddhist Tantra, one meditates on the transition states of consciousness, also called the three bodies, or *kayas*, of a Buddha.

> **Dharmakaya:** The first bardo after death is called *dharmata,* where one is liberated from the body and becomes unlimited mind. Spaciousness is its quality and in meditation, you can practice feeling as if you were floating in unlimited space.

Sambhogakaya: There is an infusion of light and radiance that comes next and one enters into feelings of complete enjoyment. This is the intermediate state before rebirth and is called the "enjoyment body" in Tantra meditation.

Nirmanakaya: This is beginning of the rebirth process and called the "emanation body."

The Process

Begin by focusing on Bodhichitta. Center your attention into your Awakened Heart. Now visualize your guru, special teacher, deity, god, or goddess. Picture your deity of choice in detail and imagine the deity directly above your Crown Chakra. See the being dissolve into light and enter your Crown Chakra and move into your heart. Feel the qualities of this being growing in you until you become the same qualities.

1. Enter into a meditation on dying and feel yourself float in the empty space of dharmakaya.
2. As you begin to reemerge from floating in space, feel the enjoyment body awaken with the feelings and awareness connected to the deity you visualized entering your heart.
3. As you reemerge even further, become the embodiment of the deity you are visualizing. Feel totally transformed into the being you worship and offer this to others.

There are detailed teachings of this path in the suggested reading list, but this should give you a flavor of Tibetan Tantra.

An Emerging Western Tantra

The West has become a melting pot of many world traditions and is the fertile seedbed where a new spirituality is being born. Traditional religions, pagan traditions, and New Age thinking are all melding together, and a Western spirituality is being born from this fertile commingling. Just as when Tantra moved into

Tibet and it assumed the images and icons of Tibetan Buddhism, the Tantra being born in the West will metamorphose into the images and icons of our culture. The West is a melting pot culture, and it is hard to tell what will emerge. Tantra is alive and well in the Western world. The excitement of the senses is something we know all about, so a spiritual teaching that celebrates the senses is certain to gain a strong foothold. Western Tantra has a highly sexual flavor, so much so that Tantra has become equated with sexual yoga in the Western mind. If we don't judge this as base and see it for what it is, we can see the beauty behind it. The sexual arena of life is where we are most hung up, and Tantric practices are needed here more than anywhere else.

The principles of Tantra are genuine, as evidenced by the successful translation of all the essential principles into Tibetan Buddhism, with a whole new mythology and pantheon of deities to support the teachings with the same core teachings intact. With the growing interest of Tantra in the West, how will the principles morph into a mythology and pantheon born of our culture?

There are those Tantric schools that are absolutely disciplined in staying away from pleasures of the flesh, and others that jump right into the fire of it. The Western world is deeply immersed in the sensual and material world and instead of changing directions to a more spiritual outlook, which has often been encouraged, perhaps the path of Tantra, which delves into the sexual and sensational aspects of life, could be appropriate.

When Shunryu Suzuki first came to America, he asked, "But where is your American Buddhism?" He saw that those who were practicing Buddhism had transplanted all of the imagery and ritual from the Orient, and he wondered where was it naturally arising out of the culture. The same question can be asked, "Where is our Western Tantra?" The pioneers of Western Tantra bring the teachings from the East, which plants the seed for what will emerge as a Western Tantra.

The word *Tantra* itself means "to weave," thus the Tantra path is to weave together all aspects of your life into your spiritual path of awakening. Osho describes Tantra as the great "Yes-sayer" of all the spiritual paths. It is the path of acceptance of the

Divine grace behind all of manifestation. Of all the paths, Tantra might be best suited for the Westerner in that it embraces a highly individualistic and experiential approach to one's growth and awakening. Most spiritual practices require sacrifice, giving up this, that, or the other in favor of God. Tantra requires no sacrifices in that all is considered sacred and you are asked to bring conscious awareness to all that you do, rather than mold your behavior to fit certain precepts.

Most of the world's religious paths seem to imply that dead is better: heaven, Nirvana, off the wheel of death and rebirth. Only Tantra acknowledges what tremendous gifts this life and this body are. Ask the dead; they seem to be lined up waiting for another chance at physical life! And the gods, the angels, the spirit guides, and the departed souls, they all want to be here. There is a tremendous pressing in on this planet from those not embodied and seeking experience on this plane.

The Tantric path looks indulgent to those who deny the gift of life and close off the senses as a spiritual path. Tantra allows you to say "yes" to life, your body, and your experiences. Tantra teaches there is a way of becoming fully awakened through life experiences, rather than denying them. Desire and pleasure are not looked down upon as the enemies of the spiritual path as they are in other traditions, they are considered Divine expressions: Worldly desire is the human reflection of the desire for God, and is courted for its life force. Pleasure is a human reflection of the indescribable state of bliss of spiritual union. Sexual union is a door to the spiritual.

The sensations of the flesh are not to be avoided or suppressed; they are to be courted for their vital storehouse of prana, the universal life force. This is not a hedonistic path however. It is not just to get lost in the base pleasures of the senses; it is to use this vital life force to awaken the kundalini. As the kundalini rises up the sushumna channel, the goddess energy floods into each successive chakra and the pleasure of the senses ultimately becomes transformed into the bliss of ecstatic union with the Divine. It is not just a one-way street of moving away from the physical and towards the spiritual; the inverse of this is also part of the path. Essentially, the Divine is invited in to experience life through the senses.

Missing Life While Searching for God

Contemplating the Tantric philosophy you come to the awareness that many of us have been missing our life while searching for God. We are taught that liberation can't be here in this existence; so many of us have renounced the world and its pleasures as the starting point of the quest. Have we thrown the proverbial baby out with the bath water? Tantra teaches that our lives are an expression of God—how could this not be? In renouncing the physical world, we are renouncing God. We are born with senses and drives that come from being in a body. To treat them anything less than Godlike is to not receive the gift. Perhaps this is the true original sin.

The trap of the sensory world, in how it can demand complete attention and limit awareness to the three dimensional plane, is still a trap in Tantra. Another of the meanings of the word Tantra is "to expand," and if there aren't practices to awaken the higher centers of consciousness, you have fallen into the trap. If the senses and the ego-centered mind consume all of your attention, you haven't expanded into higher, transcendent realms, missing a whole spectrum of consciousness and bliss that Tantra teachings reveal as available.

This is where Tantra can help with its teaching that there is no separation between God and creation. When I ask a group of modern seekers, "Where is God?" most reply that God is everywhere and in all things. Yet, individually, most of these same people who say God is everywhere often go through periods of guilt and shame about their own behavior as if they were somehow not part of God. Examine this seemingly humble behavior, "God is everywhere and in all things, except me." It starts off sounding humble, as in, "I'm not deserving of God's grace." In reality, is there a more arrogant statement? It is as if they are saying, "There are only two realities: God, which makes up everything outside of me; and me, the second reality that stands outside of God."

The goal of Tantra is not to deny life to find God, but to embrace this life as God's gift. The big draw of Tantra is what this philosophy opens up in terms of sexuality, but a Tantric lifestyle would spread out to all aspects of life, since all of creation is God and meant to be experienced as such.

With Tantra, you open up to both the physical and spiritual at once. You don't repress the ego, you engage the ego, but you keep it within its own realms. The first three chakras deal with matters concerning the ego- and body-centered consciousness. Remembering the first law of Tantra, creator and creation are one, the body and its natural drives and urges are not to be avoided; the body is sacred and its drives are sacred when sacred awareness is brought into the activity. Since the world is not the illusionary trappings of Maya, it is seen instead as the expression of love from the dance of Shiva and Shakti, thus all is available for Divine activity.

There is no division between God and Devil in Tantra, just God. There is no Maya to explain an illusionary world—all that is, is an expression of the Divine dance of Shiva and Shakti—no separation between the profane and the Divine. Every experience is an opportunity for awakening, nothing to prepare for, just now. Whatever will be then, is the same as now; Saṃsara and Nirvana are one. It is going to be the same on the other side, so we might as well get it right, right here and now.

There is no division between God and Devil in Tantra, just God.

Awareness Is

Tantra has always existed on the fringe of the religions of India, being much too radical for convention. However, all of the negative judgments about the Tantra path from orthodox Hinduism have not stopped its appeal or impact. At first it is easy to dismiss this rejection of Tantra from the mainstream as simply Victorian values in another garb, but there is appropriate caution concerning this path, which can easily become as indulgent as it is accused of being. What is the distinction between indulgence and awakening? Awareness. Simply engaging in sexuality, or other pleasurable activities, is not Tantra unless there is awareness, unless you invite God in. Georg Feuerstein says it well: "Tantra is a dangerous path that leads fools into greater bondage and only wise practitioners into freedom and bliss."[2]

Awareness. Becoming aware of each moment. The observer and the performer become as one. Life will call, natural drives will stimulate activities for the performer, but is the observer constantly attentive? This is the fruit of Tantra—Heaven and Earth both coexist in each moment. Stay attentive to the observer, the witness, the point of awareness through all experiences, and the fruit ripens.

That's it. It is awareness that makes an experience a Tantra experience. Tantra is the path of constantly expanding awareness, entering into life experiences, but always with awareness—awake and attentive on as many levels at once as you can be. Tantra is born out of the same Hindu teachings that explore the seven chakras as seven distinct levels of consciousness available. Tantra seeks to light up all seven at once. You assume they are already operating and you approach life as if they were, expanding your consciousness into all seven simultaneously. You bring God to your experiences. You don't assume you can hide from God anyway, nor that God will only be there for you if you act in certain ways. How could God not be there? Instead of doing certain things to bring God to your life, you assume God is always present and you expand your awareness to include this, after all, where isn't God?

The Kali age that we are now in brings strong drives for the experiences of the physical world. Instead of battling these drives as if they were evil, Tantra says why not use these natural drives and bring awareness into the experience? This tremendously expands the field of possibilities for the spiritual seeker. The Kali Yuga also brings forth the shadow side of humanity, and many will go through dark experiences, such as abuse and violence. Awareness can be born even in the darkest of places for practitioners of Tantra, thus they don't carry around the feeling of being damaged goods. So much of the difficulty in dealing with abuse and so forth comes from dealing with the shame. There are no shameful experiences in Tantra, just human experiences and opportunities to grow in awareness.

From the I Ching: "It is only when we have the courage to face things exactly as they are, without any sort of deception or illusion, that a light will develop out of events, by which a path to success may be recognized."[3] Shame won't help; it only distorts perception.

Religions often leave us feeling guilty and ashamed of our humanness. "I am working on becoming more spiritual and often I fall off the path and act so human, I just hate myself in these moments." How many times have we all heard this? What if we already are spiritual beings—how do you work on becoming something that you already are? If God is omnipresent, how could you act in a way that is outside of everything? If everything that you do or think is part of God's creation, how can you act in a non-Godly way? How would you act if you carried God in your heart now?

Regaining Your Purity

Many of us will experience abuse, abandonment, and betrayal during the Kali Yuga—it comes with the territory. Religions that carry strong moral codes foster feelings of guilt and shame from these encounters. Many people spend a lifetime in therapy dealing with the moral wounds of life. In the Kali Yuga, we are referring to a huge portion of the population. The Tantric path offers a viable alternative. Osho teaches: "He who follows Tantric precepts while making love becomes a virgin." The Tantric path allows you to regain your purity. By engaging the higher centers of consciousness, which are not incarnated with the ego identity, you get in touch with a part of your character that has never been wounded by life.

Spirit is never wounded, sick, tired, and so forth. The ego goes through these experiences, but not your original spirit. Tantra leads you to affirming your Divine nature. There is no separation between the profane and the spiritual: every experience provides an opportunity for awakening. It is tough to see the spiritual perspective in violent or abusive experiences one may have gone through, but who knows what spiritual benefit might be there? An opportunity to burn off karma? An opportunity that forces you to develop compassion for human weakness, whether it is in you or another? An opportunity to practice nonattachment—are you a product of your experiences so that you have to hold on to them to affirm your identity? Or, are you an eternal being going through life experiences, but not accumulating them? Who knows what spiritual illumination is there, but it is there, available even in the darkest of times.

Who knows what each of us will learn from any given experience? No one can effectively read another person's karma. This is highly individualistic, and why the Tantra path is not for the timid. You don't get consensus feedback that you are doing it right. It takes courage to face life lessons alone, but this is a shortcut to awakening. Going with consensus view, you evolve right along with the pace of your church or group with whom you are aligned. With Tantra, you don't try to mold your behavior to any moral precepts outside of self—you take life head-on and experience it directly, rather than through a filter of how it should be. Thus, every experience holds a lesson, specifically tailored for you.

Those whose spiritual path includes strong moral sanctions concerning right and wrong behavior look strongly askance at the Tantra lack of moral code. True, there are many followers of the right-hand path of Tantra who live a life of strict discipline of purification and ritual with strong moral codes of right behavior. However, a Tantric seeker develops moral qualities, not from following rules, but from the natural blossoming of human consciousness when it awakens to the spiritual and transcendent levels.

A Tantric seeker develops moral qualities, not from following rules, but from the natural blossoming of human consciousness when it awakens to the spiritual and transcendent levels.

You Can't Get There From Here

Tantra teachings have always been shrouded in secrecy, even purposefully, with the belief that it would be dangerous if the teachings were to fall into the wrong hands. Here the sanctions are redundant. The first level of awakening beyond an ego-encapsulated view of life is the Heart Chakra and the heartfelt awareness that we are all in this together. Compassion and love are the flowering of the Awakened Heart and this is the built in safeguard to the higher levels of consciousness. You can't get to the upper chakras and the transcendent levels of consciousness other than through the Heart Chakra—the Awakened Heart. It is the doorway and the foundation of the upper chakras. You can experience the upper chakras without an Awakened Heart, but in order to sustain the higher-level energy, a balanced Fourth Chakra must be the foundation.

Another built-in safeguard to the Tantra tradition is this: those who would misuse the energy of higher consciousness for personal gain are extending the ego into realms it is not meant for. When the ego interferes with the energy of the upper chakras, it distorts and deflects the higher energy from its true course. This grasping of the ego for that which is beyond its nature creates personal karma. The imbalance this reveals will be in the person's energy field, and he or she will attract situations that force attention on the imbalanced chakra, pulling energy away from the higher energy of the upper chakras. We each make our own karmic bed. Misusing higher consciousness energy for personal gain creates its own karma.

Take Refuge in Your Heart

The path of the heart liberates one from fear and all those who would exploit us with fear. Love is the strongest force in the world. This is not just a nice Sunday school saying, it is a powerful truth. When you anchor yourself in your heart, you become impervious to fear. It has no place to grab hold in you.

When you experience loss of direction or meaning in your life, learn to take refuge in your heart. You learn that love is the strongest power in the world—there is no darkness that can put out the light of love. When you are uncertain, center yourself in your heart and trust that anything born out of love will be in your best interest. Focusing your attention on your Heart Chakra dispels worry and uncertainty. Not that issues are solved, instead, you rise above needing everything to be solved. Finding your center in uncertain times is no small trick, but uncertain times punctuate a truth that is always present: uncertainty, impermanence, and change are the norms that we all live by, with a few stable moments, like eddies in a river that keeps on flowing endlessly.

To awaken your Heart Chakra, count your blessings, focus on someone or something that you love (person, plant, animal, or mineral), be generous, and give something to someone. Engage life.

A Heart Chakra Meditation

First, imagine your heart to be like a cup or chalice and make sure it is right-side up. Now, focus on all the people that you have loved and those who have loved you. When you feel the warmth of this energy, picture it as filling your heart cup. Now focus on beauty that you remember experiencing recently, or in distant memory. When you feel the uplifting energy of the beauty, fill your cup with this energy. Now focus on the Divine ones: Jesus, Buddha, Divine Mother, guardian angels, however you picture those that help us from the spiritual realms. Fill your cup with this energy, too. Now picture your heart pumping this energy through your entire being and bathe in this warmth. Ah, the Awakened Heart!

The Subtle Realms

As you stay present with awareness anchored in the Heart Chakra, you begin to have flashes of insight from the Fifth Chakra, located at the throat. You begin to have access to the universal mind. This higher-level mental energy gives flashes of insight, sudden knowing, and an awakened intuition, allowing you to access information from direct knowing. Different than thinking something through and coming to a conclusion, it is spontaneous knowing. If you can stay mindful that this is not the ego's territory, you won't try to store up and safeguard insights gained from the universal mind. This would be taking individual possession of the ideas and insights, evidence that the ego is at hand. Better to creatively express them and share them with the world, thus the Fifth Chakra deals with expression. Not just expression as in simply talking, this is creative expression, born out of merging with the universal mind.

Awakening to the Sixth Chakra, the third eye at the brow, gives you the ability to rise far above earthly issues and into the transcendent realms. In the yogic traditions, withdrawing the senses from the worldly realm, pratyahara facilitates this deep meditation. Tantra, however, is not only transcendent, but also integrative, and offers the path of simultaneous expression in both the transcendent and the worldly. God is both transcendent and imminent. Where is not God? In the transcendent practices you picture the point of awareness rising above the separate individual and into the transcendent spiritual realms. With Tantra, we can include the image of the transcendent, spiritual realm piercing the realm of the separate individual, infusing the self and the body with Divine essence.

An analogy of this could be interpenetrating waves, like at the mouth of a river where it empties into the ocean. The river extends itself and flows into the ocean where it will be absorbed. The ocean also extends into the river, particularly at high tide. The self flows into God; God flows into the self.

Drawing From the Ocean of Bliss

It is not about effort; that is why it is so important to start where you are. Making effort to change your life is making effort. This goes along with the view that spiritual benefits come through effort, as if it were something to achieve. The Tantric view of bliss *(ananda)* can be quite refreshing. Bliss exists, in and of itself. It is not something to achieve or create; it already exists. We exist in a Divine ocean of bliss and it is yours to tap into. It exists a priori, not when you make it happen. All one needs to do is draw on it, invite bliss in. Sensations stimulate the energy that can rise from within to drink the sweet nectar of the Divine.

In our Western traditions, we are familiar with Divine Grace, seen as God intervening in our lives, even though we are sinners and undeserving. Grace is the outpouring of a compassionate God, be it protection or unmerited gifts. Tantra removes "undeserving" and "unmerited." With the Tantra philosophy, you can move into the subtle and spiritual realms with confidence, knowing this is your Divine heritage.

As you continue to expand your awareness and awaken to the third-eye level of consciousness, you receive the flow of inspiration that comes from the ability to listen to inner guidance and the transcendent realms. This is a knowing beyond knowing. With the Fifth Chakra, the energy has a decidedly mental flavor; the Sixth Chakra is beyond the mind, and into images. The artist and the spiritual seeker both skillfully use this ability to imagine, drawing inspiration from a source beyond the ego. From the awakened Sixth Chakra, you are able to perceive the hidden currents of the Tao; you can commune with guides and teachers, and enter into a type of knowing beyond knowledge. You are able to rise above all polarity and experience a unitive state of consciousness, which sees all polarity as contained in the dance of a larger reality. The still quiet voice within becomes your point of reference. Tantric practitioners are able to gain profound wisdom through higher states of meditation.

If the ego gets involved with the imagery of the third eye, it begins to use the imagination for its own benefit as in sexual fantasy and illusions of all sorts. Even incessant fear is the bending of the imagination to that which is fearful to the ego . . . again, ego-directed. Illusions upon illusions are the never-ending doings of the ego, imagining things to be the way the ego wants them to be; not how they are. This leads to endless cycles of illusion/delusion and back again. It definitely takes training not to fall prey to the ego's influence and bending of the true inspirational guidance that does come through the awakened Sixth Chakra. This is why most traditions teach a quieting of the ego as a necessary step in listening to the still quiet voice within. We can readily see the wisdom behind the intent.

A familiar example of the ego's distortion of truth can be seen in infatuation relationships. Many a great friendship has been ruined by the ego misinterpreting the signals from another. Perhaps there is a good rapport being established at the friendship level and possibly even a good soul connection between two individuals. If one of the individuals misinterprets the warmth as a come-on, the friendship often ends in disaster.

Tantra, however, does not believe in simply quieting the ego and the body-centered level of consciousness. The body and its senses are vehicles of the Divine expression and doorways to get to know the Divine, thus they are to be treated as such, and not simply quieted. Tantra teaches integration. Can you be alive, awake, and attentive in the sensory realm, and simultaneously be watching this involvement from the detached observer perspective of the Sixth Chakra? Can you not only bring consciousness, but also sacredness to all of your life activities? This is not the path of renunciation; instead we could call it "involved awareness." In the above example, with involved awareness, the individual could enjoy the delight of the magnetism shared in the friendship, but not become attached to it nor try to make it something other than what it is.

The ten-thousand-petalled lotus flower is the image of the awakened Crown Chakra. The blossoming of Divine consciousness is experienced as ecstatic bliss. In the yogic traditions this is reached through meditation at its highest level—Samahdi, absorption into God. The Tantra path also leads to this deepest state of Divine absorption, but being integrative, seeks to achieve this level of consciousness while simultaneously being in the world. This is not the ego supplicating itself to God; this is the ego and God rejoicing together. The ego inviting in the God presence becomes God expressed as man or woman. The

This is not the ego supplicating itself to God; this is the ego and God rejoycing together.

bumper stickers that ask "What would Buddha do?" or "What would Jesus do?" gets right to the point. You merge with your image of the Divine so that the Divine is experiencing life through you.

This Precious Human Existence

Tantra, like Buddhism and Hinduism, teaches the importance of understanding "this precious human existence." Although rebirth will surely happen for all but the rarest few souls, there is no guarantee you will incarnate in human form again. There are other possibilities from the animal kingdom to the realm of the gods. But it is only from the human realm that final enlightenment is possible. Even the gods must first reincarnate in human form to reach final enlightenment. It is easy to suspect anthropomorphism—it is, after all, humans that came up with this view. But, none the less, the teachings aren't another round of "We're number one!" Instead, they remind us not to waste this precious existence. Awaken to the fullness of your birth potential in both the physical and spiritual realms—in this life, in this day.

This plane and in this body is where we can experience the full seven chakras. While not in a body, it is easy to stay in the transcendent realms (that is where you are), but not possible to experience the sensory realms of the body. While in a body, you have the same transcendent capacity through the upper chakras as those who are not embodied, but you also have the lower chakras of the body and its senses. This is more than, not less than. This is expanded potential, not limited potential.

True, if people remain trapped in the confines of the ego-encapsulated view of life (the lower chakras), they are cut off from the transcendent realms. But, if one is able to grow in consciousness while simultaneously experiencing the fullness of this life, this is expanded awareness. It is also true that the ferociousness of the ego should not be underestimated. Its tenacious grip on maintaining its position as the center of your attention must be dealt with in some way, or awareness will be limited to the ego's range.

Spiritual Practices

Spiritual practices liberate us from the ego's grasping and redirect attention to the higher realms. In the Tantra tradition these include meditation, mantra chanting, yantras (creating and contemplating mandala-like drawings which reveal the interpenetration and integration of the physical and spiritual), and mudras (postures for the hands and body, to invoke a certain deity). These work. They work because they are sound spiritual practices that anchor one's attention in the higher realms. Are they the only and specific formula? I don't believe so.

What is the intent behind the practices? To break the grip of the ego-centered mind and liberate awareness to the spiritual planes. The Tantra techniques work well for those who are drawn to these practices. But if you already have a practice, and know the way beyond the ego, then you are already there.

This is not renouncing the validity of the Tantra tradition of very specific techniques as to number of times to chant a specific mantra, the pronunciation of the syllables, or what specific yantras drawn in a specific manner to invoke a specific deity and so forth. The right-hand path of Tantra is very disciplined and has a long lineage of adepts and realized beings that stand testimony to the validity of this path. But I don't think one must submit to this rigorous path, unless you are so inclined. There must be some practice, technique, or method for shifting your attention away from the ego's chattering. Otherwise you might become at peace with listening to your ego and its musings, and missing out on the transcendent.

Thus, meditation, in one guise or another, is required, but if you already are on a path that includes mediation and truly does liberate you from the ego's grasp, you do not need to discard your proven techniques to practice Tantra. After all, where isn't God? If we remember the premise that all is God, then it wouldn't be just one specific formula that could invoke the Divine presence. But without effort and attention, the ego will prevail and dominate your awareness.

Why Spiritual Disciplines?

The question arises, "If it is all God, then why go through spiritual disciplines and practices?" The question has some validity. If it is all God, then what does it matter what you are doing with your life? Here, two issues are important. First, getting pulled into the sensory-gratification mode and calling it spirituality is a huge trap. Tantra removes the barriers between sacred and profane, true, but getting lost in the senses and losing the perspective of the Divine is just as much of a test in Tantra as it is in all human experiences. You must at all times maintain perspective of the Divine during the experience to truly be Tantra.

The second issue is that the disciplines and practices exercise a part of your character that lies dormant without attention. The higher centers of awareness require a shift of attention to gain their vantage point. This is why the disciplines are there, because they are tools for helping shift attention to higher-level awareness. This shift can happen without discipline, and does. Those rare magic moments, often in nature, when your energy spontaneously shifts into higher-level awareness and you see everything in your life from a whole new perspective. These are perhaps the best, but again, they are rare, thus the disciplines are used to purposefully shift one's attention.

Engaging in the sexual and sensory realms without discipline and practice of some sort to awaken the higher states of consciousness, and calling it Tantra is just indulgence by another name. But, is it the specific exercises that Tantra practitioners perform that lead to higher awareness? Not necessarily. The practices work because they are good, effective spiritual practices. But throughout this book we've run across many good, effective spiritual practices, and as long as you are practicing something to shift your energy and you actually reach the realms of higher awareness, that is the point of the traditional Tantra practices.

The body is honored as a vehicle for the Divine, and purification practices and Hatha Yoga are used to transform the body to sustain the higher-level, yet subtle, spiritual energy. Focusing on the body as a vessel of Divine energy, it can only be helpful to refine the energies of the body through exercise, diet, and meditation/spiritual practices. But these disciplines should not be used as a measure of your spirituality. When you fall off your discipline (you will, we do), remember: God is here, too. Consciousness work doesn't stop when you have fallen; these are often exquisite opportunities for awakening. And awakening is what it is all about.

One of my favorite sayings is "Enlightened today, asshole tomorrow." Although crude, there is a truth to the saying. A spiritual path of awakening is not a constant, one-way direction. It is more often characterized by "two steps forward, one step backward." On the path of awakening, we can be so clear, loving, and compassionate one day, and such jerks the next! But these days of falling off the path can also facilitate tremendous awareness if you are paying attention.

I remember coming back home from one of my first yoga retreat weekends. During the retreat, I was at my spiritual best and left the weekend feeling quite elevated and spiritual. Upon returning home, I found myself craving beer and got quite intoxicated. Things quickly degenerated and I picked a fight with my wife and said some really nasty things to her. And if that wasn't bad enough, her sister and her children were visiting, so I not only humiliated myself, I did it publicly, with plenty of witnesses.

The physical hangover I experienced the next day was nothing to the "dark night of the soul" I was experiencing from my behavior. However, the depression forced some honest self-evaluation of where I was really at on my path and how that fit with my indulgent behavior. This dark night experience did as much for me on my path of awakening as any inspired spiritual talk I have attended.

Disciplines are necessary, but when spiritual disciplines become militaristic, they harden one's character, rather than soften it. The point of meditation and spiritual practice is to soften the heart and open to a spacious awareness. If you get too focused on the discipline, it can create rigidity. Ram Dass teaches that all methods are traps. You need a method for liberation, but as soon as you become attached to the method, you become trapped by it, effectively blocking the very liberation you seek. Osho teaches that methods are the fingers pointing to the moon. When you get too focused on finger positioning, you lose sight of the moon.

This is the wisdom of having many methods to draw from. When one method has become stale, instead of holding on to empty ritual, void of spirit, you refresh your search for spirit by using another method in your medicine bag of spiritual resources. The eclectic path is sometimes looked down upon as noncommittal. However, for the Tantric seeker, the commitment is to awakening, not the method.

This is inviting God into your belly rather than transcending your belly to be with God. This is the revolution of Tantra. Don't be different than who you are; hide from nothing, but bring God with you into every experience. It is like offering yourself as a vehicle for God to gather sensory experiences. The discipline is not to repress the ego; rather it is to blur the distinction between the ego and God. This is God doing what you do. Accept this premise and stay mindful of it and your life will transform. Not because you are disciplining it to transform, but because it naturally does when you invite the Divine into your life. This interpenetration of the ego and Divine creates its own alchemical process and you start becoming more conscious, aware, and loving.

Tantra: ***To weave. To weave the Divine into your life and your life into the Divine.***

There is no thought you can have, no experience you can have, that does not have God present. You can't hide from the omnipresent. Just bringing this awareness into all that you do, without changing anything, brings changes into which activities you will allow into your life.

Joel Goldsmith, a Christian mystic, often said it this way, "God, Is, As, One." God, what else can be said, it is all God. There is aliveness to life and God that goes on whether concepts agree with it or not. This is not something to be learned as if it existed in some distant time and far-away place. The is-ness of life is right in front of our eyes. God as _____; whatever you say next, this is

God as a basketball game, a sacred ceremony, a fight, a pigeon, or anything else you can consider. If it's all God, it's all God. One; the essential unity of all life. From the Vedas, "There is but one truth, although the sages will call it by many names." One.

The Initiation

The traditional Tantra adept goes through an initiation with a guru to set him on the Tantric path. In the Buddhist tradition this is called an "empowerment"; in the Hindu tradition it is called shaktipat; it is the same quickening in both traditions. As part of the initiation, the guru awakens the kundalini of the initiate leading to states of awareness and bliss never before experienced. This sets the course for the initiate: He knows where he is going—he has been there. This awakened Shakti energy will continue to awaken and purify the initiate's inner vision. This "piercing" by the guru is a bit like a jump-start, or priming the pump that sets the initiate on his or her path.

The guru tradition has not done well in the West. This absolute surrender to another being as if it were Shiva himself doesn't fit well with the Western temperament. Just the huge number of true seekers and the precious few number of realized beings available makes this one-to-one transmission inaccessible to many. If you are so blessed as to have found a true teacher/guru, this is indeed a blessing, but for many of us, we don't want to be left out of the teaching just because tradition says you have to have direct transmission from a guru. I am sure it is a valid way, but if you haven't found a guru, don't let this stop your quest.

Consider the principle at work in guru-disciple transmission. The guru is said to be an expression of Shiva. The disciple is not simply surrendering to an ordinary being; he must believe the guru can be as Shiva for him. All-knowing. All-loving. All-consuming. The guru is the spiritual teacher who knows just what the disciple needs to continue on the path of awakening.

If you are not of the guru type, or have simply not found your teacher, can you find alternative methods for activating the principles of the guru? Can you find a way to surrender to God as all knowing, all loving and all consuming? The guru serves as a focusing point for this surrender to Shiva. If not a guru, then what is it for you that you can absolutely surrender to? God? Jesus? Buddha? Kali? Shakti? The Tao? There are other ways to focus this surrendering, but this principle of surrendering to a larger reality must be met in order to continue to expand beyond ego-centered consciousness.

The principle of experiencing accelerated growth by being in the presence of a realized being is not as easy to come across, but by examining the principle, you can find ways to employ this. The guru tradition works for those who find the rare true teacher who is also willing to have them as disciples. It works because the principle works—being in the presence of high beings stimulates a higher level of awareness in you by sympathetic resonance. The higher vibration that these beings are emanating awakens your own ability to rise above the muck in your life and see things from a higher perspective.

Being in the presence of a realized being is like hearing a tuning fork that awakens previously dormant levels of awareness. I recently had the great good fortune to meet His Holiness, the Dalai Lama, face-to-face. This was at a reception and my encounter was brief—only a matter of seconds, time enough to meet him and receive a blessing. These few seconds catalyzed a level of awareness in me that lasted for several days. It was not all pleasant. There was a euphoric high, true, but the expanded awareness allowed me to see parts of my character in a new light that was not all that flattering.

This is what high beings can do for you—they set you on your path. Not by telling you what you need to do, but by catalyzing your own higher awareness. Tantra masters come in all shapes and sizes, and you wouldn't necessarily know one by appearance, or lifestyle. You know by their energy and how you feel in their presence. We all have people in our life who, just being with them, not only lifts our spirits but also expands our awareness; start there.

Take advantage of opportunities to experience the high teachings and teachers. If you are not the type to seek out a specific guru, activate the guru principle anyway. Seek out the teachings and the teachers who operate on a higher vibration. Going to hear the teachers speak when they come to town, reading the books and listening to the tapes, attending workshops, retreats, and seminars. This works well.

Ah, the teachings! Thank God for the teachings. The teachings and the teachers might very well be the guru for the Western seeker. One of the great gifts of our time is the availability of the teachings in books and on tape. The trials and tribulations seekers of days gone by must have had to put up with to get the teachings—now we can listen to the great teachers of the world on audiocassette in our car! True, we are not getting the Shaktipat of being in their presence, but the access to the high-quality teachings is tremendous and some of the higher vibrations are transmitted through the teachers' voices and words . . . even on tape and in books. Adepts on all paths spend regular time studying the scriptures. What are the scriptures for you? What information inspires you and illumines your soul? Spend time with the teachings and teachers whether it is through books, tapes, classes or individual instruction.

Changing Behavior Through Tantra (To Repress Something Makes It Stronger)

The forbidden fruit tastes sweetest is the teaching here. That which we push down and attempt to repress only gets stronger. It doesn't go away, it lies in wait for a moment when the discipline of self-control is at its weakest and then it comes back in full force, and we're back to our old routines. Most of us are all too familiar with this pattern. Tantra offers an alternative route. Take part in the experience you are drawn to, but do it with absolute awareness. If it is something you've outgrown, you'll have the experience, become aware of its lack of value and that is that. By hiding the behavior from our awareness we have to compartmentalize our self-awareness, separating conflicting beliefs and behavior patterns. When in the pull of a habit, it is as if your self-awareness goes temporarily numb. This creates a schism in consciousness, the opposite of what Tantra teaches.

Letting Behaviors Drop (When They No Longer Serve You)

Tantra would offer a different approach to quitting a behavior. Let's say an obvious one, like smoking. People trying to quit smoking know all the arguments and reasons; it is not that they haven't heard them before. Instead of trying to quit, the Tantric way would begin to smoke with conscious awareness. Make a ritual out of it—treat it special. With Tantric sex we are encouraged to approach our lover as a god or goddess to bring out the sacred in the experience. What can you do with smoking to make it a ritualistic encounter with the Divine? Native Americans brought ritualistic consciousness to their tobacco ceremonies. Bring full awareness to the act. Habits are largely unconscious behavior patterns. Bringing conscious awareness to that which once was unconscious changes the experience altogether.

Swami Muktananda tells the story in *Play of Consciousness*. While he was still with other disciples with his guru, he was singled out by his teacher as having special gifts. He was instructed to go off to a private hut and spend his time in meditation to prepare for his next initiation. Muktananda was filled with pride and set out in earnest to follow his assignment. He was making wonderful progress in his meditations and experienced many ecstatic states of consciousness.

However, it wasn't long before he began to have sexual fantasies and he was constantly interrupted in his meditations by the image of a provocative lady dancing before his inner vision. Muktananda was following a celibate path, thus sexual fantasy was not suitable meditation practice. He tried to shake the image, but she would not leave. At first he was annoyed, but when it went on for days and weeks, he became quite disturbed. He didn't even dare sleep for fear that he would surrender to the seductress in his sleep.

He couldn't meditate. He couldn't sleep. Feeling totally dejected, he was ready to admit defeat. Filled with shame for not being the great being his guru thought him to be, he went to admit his failure. Dejectedly, he sought advice from a great teacher, who upon hearing of Muktananda's woes, told him this was Kundalini Shakti and a sign that he would be able to give Shaktipat to others in the future. He further told him that the naked woman was from his own repressed images of woman, and if he would look upon her as the goddess Chiti, he would receive a Divine blessing from her.

Muktananda went back to his meditation hut, allowed the fantasy, but related to her as the Divine Mother dancing before him. This transformed the lust into Divine Bliss. He also went on to be the great teacher his guru thought him to be, establishing the Siddha Yoga Foundation, which still has a following worldwide.[4]

The story is a Tantra story and its applications are profound. Whatever you do, do it with awareness. If it is smoking, instead of sneaking a smoke, as if you could hide from God, smoke in full awareness. Bring God to your smoking. Smoke and feel the sensations totally, and experience this as if God were experiencing it. Stay completely aware of the whole experience, the good and the bad. Feel the rush of energy that comes from the nicotine and smell the smell of tobacco on your skin. What is the taste of the smoke in your mouth? What is the sensation in your chest and lungs? As you bring full awareness to your smoking, you stay with it while it serves you, but there will come a time when it no longer serves you. There will come a time when the benefits are outweighed by the detriments, and then the behavior drops of its own accord. You are not tying to quit; it simply drops because it is no longer serving you.

With overeating it is the same thing. When you try to push the behavior down, it becomes stronger. You find yourself gulping food as if you could sneak it past the one who is watching. Eat in full awareness. Bring your full awareness to every bite, feel the sensations of taste. Slow down your experience of eating and experience the full taste of each bite. What happens? Satiation comes easier. Instead of sneaking this past your awareness, bring your awareness to it and you will find that satisfaction comes sooner, fullness is felt, and the need for overeating subsides.

Tantra Burns Off Karma

The Tantra path burns off karma, at least when it is not being abused and creating more karma! You become authentic by burning through your desires and fantasies, satiating them with conscious awareness. This process of deep acceptance unifies and integrates consciousness. It is present and alert at both levels simultaneously.

Tantra does not consider desire to be the evil that other traditions judge it to be. By following through on the desires that arise, and doing so with awareness, you burn off your karma. When there is a repressed desire, even though not acted upon, it still creates karma. When these desires are acted upon with awareness they tend to complete themselves never to rise again. The first layer of desire to be burned away is socially induced desire, that which your culture waves in front of your ego, enticing its cravings. When you experience the samplings of culturally induced desire with awareness, you quickly learn how temporary the satisfaction is, and this type of desire drops of its own accord.

In our culture, materialism is the name of the game, and new cars, clothes, and thingamajigs are taunted as the way to happiness. This taunts our desires for objects and all of us are familiar with the "I just have to have a new ______ to be really happy" phenomenon. How long does it last? It is always temporary to soon be replaced by the next desire. Bringing conscious awareness to this liberates you from its grasp.

Other false desires like a pay raise, promotion, improved sex life, and whiter teeth, none of which can possibly lead to ultimate happiness, are also burned through when allowed with awareness. What is left is the deeper desire of the soul to be at one with God. Where the Hindu traditions teach that even this desire must be transcended to find truth, Tantra teaches that this desire of the soul to be with God is the affirmation of God's presence, it is the experience of God, so it is not looked down upon, but honored.

Tantra Sex

Simply said, Tantra sex is making love with your partner at all levels simultaneously—the physical, emotional, mental, and spiritual. Sexual union is the perfect metaphor for emulating the

Divine couple, Shiva and Shakti. It is the ecstatic bliss of divine union that is sought, not simply enhanced pleasure. The physical pleasure of lovemaking is ultimately transformed to the ecstatic bliss of union with the Divine and the dance of the delightful bodies. The senses are used to taunt and tease the kundalini into awakening.

Tantra reverses the flow of normal attention. Your senses are awakened and could consume all of your attention, but you reverse the flow, causing the kundalini, and your attention, to rise upward and inward. You both continue to trace the awakening dance of kundalini as it rises within, and weaves through each other's chakras as well. Your lovemaking is a dance at all levels.

If it is not lovemaking, it's not Tantra. One could practice all the breathing techniques, postures, and mantras connected to Tantra, but without love, it is still simply sex. Perhaps enhanced and prolonged, but still sex.

Having Sex or Making Love

Sex must be rooted in love, or it will not blossom into the spiritual awakening of true Tantra. The first three chakras of the body can respond to sex in and of itself. For the upper chakras to be awakened, the kundalini first must pass through the Heart Chakra, your heart must open; love must be present. The first step in Tantra sexuality is to know the difference between having sex and making love. Sex is a biological urge of the body—it is instinctual as a built-in necessity to perpetuate the species. Sex can happen without love. Even with someone you love, there are times when you might not feel the love, but the body can perform sexually, essentially servicing your partner's sexual needs. Making love is altogether different and is the building block of all Tantra sexuality.

Making love transforms the physical aspect of sex into the deeply healing and transformative experience of intimacy. Intimacy is the experience of knowing and being known at the deepest level. All walls come down and putting vulnerability on the line, you learn to surrender to the experience. Making love brings in the heart and courts the heart of the other. Making love brings sweetness to the moment. Passion is just as present as it is with physical sex, but in lovemaking, there is sensitivity to each other's needs and a deep exchange of energy that can be absent in sex. With Tantra, you find pleasure by bringing out the pleasure in your partner.

In Tantra sexual practices, you learn of the feminine path to sexuality. It is important to distinguish between male/female and masculine/feminine. The energies being spoken of are not gender oriented—both male and female have masculine and feminine energy; the yin and yang is there in all of us. Since it is not gender oriented, it is also not exclusively heterosexual and encompasses all forms of magnetic love.

The goddess energy is courted by slowing down, approaching each other as if your lover were a goddess, or a god; staying in sacred awareness, and being with the energy, rather than rushing it in anyway. The masculine has a reputation for approaching sex like the rooster in the hen yard—get the business done with and move on. Not the most romantic image, and certainly not Tantric. The feminine energy rises slower and sustains longer compared to the quick rising, and equally quick finishing, masculine energy. The goddess energy is activated through forming a relationship with the energy, rather than running to the top of the mountain and jumping off.

You approach your lover by first honoring the sacredness of the opportunity. Pray, meditate, and awaken to the deep place within, and then approach your lover as if he is Shiva and she is Shakti. The goddess path is not to just experience the energy, but to form a relationship with it. This requires staying aware. The pull of the senses can completely capture all of your attention, and then it is simply sexual. To stay mindful and aware with the witness observing while you are engaged sexually is the ideal. To stay mindful you note the quality of energy within yourself, you become aware of your lover's energy, and you pay particular attention to the combined energy.

Approach your lover by first honoring the sacredness of the opportunity. Pray, meditate, and awaken to the deep place within. Then approach your lover as if he is Shiva and she is Shakti.

The feminine path of Tantra teases the building sexual energy, rather than being seized by it. The non-Tantric masculine energy of sexuality takes control of the situation and initiates a series of escalating steps towards passion as if it were competition of who can get there first. Finishing first doesn't get the prize in this game. The second rule of Tantra is to slow down. Don't stop or limit; simply slow down. This happens naturally by maintaining awareness during the sexual experience. However, maintaining awareness during sex doesn't come naturally, you have to discipline yourself to maintain the vantage point of the witness, and in sex the senses are so strong it is most easy to get totally drawn into the sensations. In Tantra, yes, you are meant to fully experience the beauty of the senses while simultaneously staying in mindful awareness of courting and exchanging energy with your lover at the emotional, mental, and spiritual levels as well.

This is Tantra sexuality. It goes on and on from here with various techniques, postures, breaths, visualizations, and so forth to enhance the experience, but this is the core of Tantra sexuality. Learning how to make love with God and your partner simultaneously.

The feminine path courts the energy and focuses on the other—tuning in and responding to your partner's energy as if it were a dance. It is not exclusively feminine, without the masculine energy there would be no polarity, no magnetism. The masculine energy has to be there in equal measure, but since it tends to dominate and take over the experience, we focus on the feminine and hold the masculine with some restraint. Again, not because the feminine is better, but because it takes this effort to bring balance to the feminine/masculine energy dance within yourself.

Reversing the Flow

Just as in Taoist sexuality, sexual fluids, particularly semen, is thought to be both the sacred elixir and our most potent life-generating force. In typical sex, the focus is on the orgasm and the release of sexual fluids, ejaculation for the male. With Tantra, ejaculation is considered to be a dissipation of the life force, and a missed opportunity to commune with the goddess. Reversal of the natural flow toward ejaculation is taught. There are books in the suggested reading section that teach the specific techniques, but basically the male reverses his attention away from ejaculation and seeks to sustain the level of excitement without letting it go over the top. Simply visualizing the vital sexual energy moving inward and upward helps.

Picture sexual energy rising to 100 percent with ejaculation. To facilitate sustaining the experience, picture holding the sexual excitement to 75–90 percent. Deep, slow breathing can assist this effort. Paying more attention to your lover's experience helps. You have to stay in mindful awareness of the witness to monitor your level of excitement. From the vantage point of the witness, redirect the flow of the energy and your attention to the awakening kundalini and its movement upward. Feel the bliss of expanded awareness as you awaken to the upper chakras. Stay mindful of your lover's kundalini rising and court it at each new level.

Stay attentive to the combined energy as well, and use this expanded energy to catapult your attention into the combined Heart Chakra. Feel the love, not only your love for each other, but also all the love that ever was and is coursing through the universe. You move into archetypal love with each other and feel the joy of all creation in response to your lovemaking. Feel that all the celestial beings are smiling and bestowing blessings upon your union. Feel the Divine dance of energy from Shiva and Shakti's lovemaking reverberate through you. Feel the descent of the Divine force as you rise up to meet it. Enter into oneness with your lover in this sacred moment.

The teachings focus a great deal on the male and this is because teaching women the path of feminine sexuality and the way to the goddess would be somewhat redundant. Since women are able to have multiple orgasms, and the sexual fluids are naturally retained within the body, the teachings are somewhat different for women. As you open to greater awareness, your ability to sustain a pre-orgasmic level of excitement is improved, just as for the male. However, this is optional. If you enjoy multiple orgasms and are able to sustain your attention on both your lover's energy and the Divine, you can choose to allow yourself to surrender to orgasm.

Allowing yourself to fully surrender to orgasm while staying mindful of your male lover's intention not to takes awareness . . . the whole point of Tantra. Picture yourself bathing in the ecstatic love of the moment at all levels, and picture your lover's energy right there with you and share your love at all levels of your being. As you take delight in the sensory experience of the moment going on within you, stay attentive to your lover at all levels as well. Know what is going on in his body as to its level of excitement. Practice the reversal of the flow of energy that naturally moves downward and out of the body. Picture the kundalini energy rising up your spine in you and your lover and your combined energy. It is a task to fully surrender to the ecstatic union and simultaneously stay attentive to the energy in your lover's body so that you don't pull him into early ejaculation.

There are extensive teachings if you are interested in further research, but this is the essence of Tantra sex. Although not commonly taught, the teachings should be somewhat age adjusted, particularly for men. Young men under the age of thirty-five are in their sexual prime and are veritable semen-making machines. The loss of vitality after ejaculation that older people speak of will be incomprehensible to young men, as the cycle of rejuvenation is extremely quick compared to what it will be down the road. So for younger men, ejaculation is not an energetic problem. Still, even for young men, the teachings of reversal of the flow have merit for slowing down the process of ejaculation and expanding the window of time to explore love's sweet embrace and your awareness into spiritual union with one another and the Divine.

Tantra Sex and the Chakras

The chakras are an essential part of many Eastern paths, but their understanding is perhaps most integral to Tantric teachings.

The First Chakra level of sex is simply biological; a physical urge that needs to be acted upon. This is lust and is built into the system of human sexuality to ensure the perpetuation of the species. The Second Chakra adds pleasure. The First Chakra is simply a biological drive, with the awakening of the Second Chakra, beauty and pleasure are brought into the act. With the awakening of the Third Chakra, power is awakened. With right intention, the will power can direct the energy to the higher Chakras. With misuse, the wills of both individuals fail to blend, and maintaining their separateness, each seeks to serve its own best interest, leading to controlling, domineering, and manipulative love. With the awakening of the Fourth Chakra, love is born and separateness dissolves. This allows the sexual experience to be transformed to a higher level. With the lower chakras, you can have sex. With the awakening of the Heart Chakra, you are making love.

With the Awakening of the Fifth Chakra, the first of the transpersonal levels of love, you go beyond the personality and your two minds together merge with the Universal Mind. With the Sixth Chakra opening, the visionary, inspirational quality of union is born. The meditative state of consciousness is entered into and shared with your partner. With the awakening of the crown or Seventh Chakra comes the full blossoming of the Tantra experience. You are experiencing the ecstatic bliss of making love with your partner and God simultaneously.

Conclusion

Although Tantra purists would chafe at such advice, Tantra is a spiritual path that wouldn't require you to change one aspect of your existing life. Many people of indulgent temperaments believe their behavior stands in the way of a spiritual life . . . the image of a spiritual life being completely contrary to the one they are living. To begin, all that is required is that you bring God with you, even into your darkest behavior. If you are going to the bar, bring Divine awareness with you. Don't change anything about your behavior patterns—just begin observing. Be in the experience and observe the experience, that's all.

This apparent license to indulge, or more accurately, license to be who you are, but with a Tantric attitude of seeing God in everything, changes your life at the pace that is appropriate for you. Let the goddess energy in; court your awakening through all that you do.

If you feel that you can't take part in spiritual practices because of the typical sanctions against indulgences, do your spiritual practices anyway. Do your yoga after the bar if you must, but do your yoga. Don't wait until you are pure. You *are* pure. Purely human—a Divine manifestation. Bring this awareness into all aspects of your human experience, hide from nothing. Bring Divine awareness into all activities, even those that are considered taboo. Whatever you are drawn to, it is still human. Don't judge your humanness. Accept even the parts of your character that you are "working" on and wish weren't there. This awareness, in and of itself, will change your life.

Tantra removes the distinction between the profane and the spiritual. This is not a path for the morally righteous—the Tantra path flaunts its ability to explore areas of life that are typically considered taboo for true spiritual seekers. Of course, the possibility of abuse runs high as all types of pleasure seeking can be justified as spiritual. Yet, aside from the abuses that surely will happen, and have happened in the name of spirituality, still the value for genuine seekers of bringing conscious awareness to all areas of life changes the nature of the experience.

"Ignorance is bliss," we are told, and this does make some sense. When you become conscious in the middle of culturally trained pleasure seeking, it often loses its attraction. For many, the sensationalism of the Western way loses some of its glitter when you become conscious in the moment and consider the full nature of the experience in front of you. At first you might find that it's a bit of a bummer to lose some of the innocent joy of pleasure seeking, but if you stay with this, after the bubbles are burst that are culturally trained images of what you should enjoy . . . after these bubbles burst, what is left is the genuine you. Then you start discovering what pleasure means to you, as you continue to weave the physical and the spiritual, accepting both, renouncing neither.

So many spiritual paths define a person as spiritual by what they don't do—what they say "no" to. "I'm spiritual because I say no to sex, alcohol, negativity, and anger." These austerities are honorable in terms of their intention, but what is the result? Often, a very bland life with no celebration, no flavor. It is not uncommon for me to sit with someone during a counseling session and hear the claim, "This is my last life on Earth." As I sit with this statement and reflect on its implications, the rejection of life that this represents becomes apparent.

The religions of the world have fostered this with teachings of, "If you are really good, you won't have to come back here to planet Earth. You will get to heaven, to Nirvana, or off the wheel of death and rebirth." What do these teachings imply about life on Earth? It is apparently not so good. If you are born, it is evidence that you have blown it on some cosmic level, or you would be free from this existence. If we were to follow these teachings to the absurd level, we could imagine people mourning the birth of a child, wearing black and lamenting that this poor incarnating soul has to suffer through another existence! But maybe, just maybe, if he is really good he won't have to come back here.

When I hear, "I won't be coming back here," I wonder what it would be like if these sincere seekers get their wish not to be reborn on Earth, and the next life they find themselves incarnated as a rock on some sulfur-ridden planet, or on some transcendent plane with vague memories of trees, flowers, gentle breezes, tender kisses, chocolate, and coffee.

Is there suffering on planet Earth? Obviously, yes. But perhaps our religions have contributed to this in the teaching that here is not good—the goal is moksha, to escape. What do these teachings have to do with the way we treat our planet and each other? Plenty. If the highest spiritual teachings suggest that being on Earth is evidence of the fall from grace, is it any wonder that we don't treat our lovely planet in a more sacred manner?

Perhaps it is time that we look at how our religions have contributed to the suffering and abuse that goes on here on planet Earth. How do we know that this is not the jewel of the entire system? Isn't it an act of extreme arrogance to be given this life on Earth and to assume that there is something better? I would think of it as the supreme cosmic joke if it turns out that being born on Earth is a great reward, and that we have received the greatest of blessings to be born here, yet, in our arrogance and ignorance, we have not seen it that way at all.

Perhaps it is time to approach life with the Tantric attitude that accepts everything in life as sacred. Where is not God? If we accepted our life on Earth as sacred, wouldn't we care for our planet and each other in an entirely different way? Perhaps we will not start treating our planet in a sacred way until our religions and spiritual paths start teaching that life is indeed a sacred gift.

The materialists, seeking pleasure through acquiring possessions and the pleasure of the senses, and the nonmaterialists, who have renounced the world and its trappings, are both being overly influenced by the material world. One in its blatant acceptance of the material world as the only thing that holds value, and the other in the denial of it. Both the excessive, and the one who denies, are immersed in their reaction to the material world. Tantra unifies, and allows practitioners to have their heads in the heaven and their feet on Earth.

After Thoughts

Tantra is bringing God to all of your experiences, rather than denying experiences to get to God. This is a whole different premise.

—David Pond

Many religions say they accept God, but not his creation. Isn't this placing self above God and judging his creation?

—David Pond

"The enlightened being, however, floats in the infinity of all desires and therefore does not have to cling to any one desire but can remain in the world, at peace, fulfilled, unattached, and yet at the same time with a relish for life in all its countless forms."[5]

—Georg Feuerstein

The Tantra path unabashedly takes part in the essential erotic nature of existence and at its highest level.

—David Pond

Mathew Fox states that it is time we snatch eroticism from the pornographers and reconnect with this in the sacred marriage. . . .

—David Pond

There are no shoulds in Tantra. There is not a way that you should be that is better that what you generally are.

—David Pond

Suggested Reading

Allen, Marcus. *Tantra for the West.* Mill Valley, Calif.: Whatever Publishing, 1981.

Feuerstein, Georg. *Tantra: the Path of Ecstasy.* Boston & London: Shambhala, 1998.

Frawley, Dr. David. *Tantric Yoga and the Wisdom Goddesses.* Salt Lake City, Ut.: Passage Press, 1994.

Gyatso, Geshe Kelsang. *Tantric Grounds and Paths.* London: Tharpa Publications, 1994.

Mumford, Dr. Jonn. *Ecstasy Through Tantra.* St. Paul, Minn.: Llewellyn Publications, 2000.

Norbu, Chogyal Namkhai. Edited by John Shane. *The Crystal and the Way of Light: Sutra, Tantra, and Dzogchen.* Ithaca, New York: Snow Lion Publications, 2000.

Osho. *Tantra: The Supreme Understanding.* Portland, Ore.: The Rebel Publishing House, year unknown.

———. *The Book of Secrets.* New York, N.Y.: St. Martin's Griffin, 1974.

Yeshe, Lama. Edited by Jonathan Landaw. *Introduction to Tantra.* Boston, Mass.: Wisdom Publications, 1987.

Endnotes

1. Sri Yukteswar is the notable exception. In *The Holy Science,* he presents a very convincing argument that we have moved out of the Kali age and have ascended to the next age, dwarpa, during the Renaissance period.
2. Feuerstein, Georg. *Tantra: The Path to Ecstasy*. p. xvi.
3. Wilhelm, Richard. *The I Ching or Book of Changes.* Translated by Cary Baynes. Hexagram #5, p. 25.
4. Muktananda, Swami. *Play of Consciousness*. pp. 88–100.
5. Feuerstein, Georg. *Tantra: The Path to Ecstasy.* p. 229.

EPILOGUE

AT THE TIME of this writing, darkness has descended upon our planet. The attack on New York, Washington, D.C., and Pennsylvania leaves little doubt that we are firmly embedded in the Kali Yuga—the Dark Age. In the Kali Yuga, humankind is said to go through its furthest descent from its spiritual source. It is not easy to keep your heart open in dark times, and that is why there is said to be special merit for spiritual behavior in the Kali age. But we must keep our hearts open if we are to heal our deep wounds.

If you are drawn to the spiritual path, realize the tremendous call to action these times herald. Spiritual workers are needed to keep the light from going out. In the wake of the recent bombings, the heroic efforts of the rescue workers to save any lives they could among the carnage stands out as a noble aspect of humanity responding to crisis.

Those on a spiritual path are the rescue workers for humanity in the Kali Yuga. Shine your light under the rubble of a collapsing material empire to be a beacon for those still trapped.

We can't stop the march of the movement toward a global community. All the major issues plaguing our modern world are global issues: environmental, economic, political, and spiritual—

it is a global issue now and it is too late to turn the tide. In individual lives, challenges are turned around once we become proactive in moving toward the solution. Life is change; change is law, the immutable truth of existence. Everything is going along just fine, and then China invades Tibet. Everything is going along just fine, and then terrorists attack. We are forced into a larger reality kicking, dragging, and screaming.

The march of evolution has moved from tribal to community, to city, to state, to country, and now stretches toward global. Just as the U.S. Civil War showed the difficulty of expanding allegiance from the state to national level, international wars are showing this same difficulty in expanding to the next level.

Is there a proactive way of moving to a global community? Of course there is, but it is overlooked in its obviousness in the Kali age. The first rule of the spiritual path is "first, do no harm," ahimsa. If we extended this to the global theater, it would encourage a coming together of different countries in a way that first does no harm. We are apparently all going to have to deal with each other, either as enemies or allies. Can we learn the way to be allies with one another, and deal with each other in ways that are mutually beneficial? That is the proactive path, as simple as it sounds. And, of course, it would work. If we were united as a global community and used our global resources to benefit and meet the needs of all the citizens, there would be prosperity, full employment (there is plenty to be done), and an improved spiritual climate to raise our children in. Too simplistic? I don't believe so, nor do I underestimate how many "civil wars" it will take until we learn that we are all in each other's best interest. Still, it is the way.

The task is enormous—to get the nations of the world to live together as one. Where to start? The military has its opinions and is strongly supported based on the horrors that we have perpetrated on one another. Here, the spiritual community of the world must unite together and see the importance of the work in front of us. There is a saying, "Let there be peace on Earth, and let it begin with me." This is where we can start, in our own lives, actualizing the teachings and demonstrating how to live in peace in the world. Our individual families and communities are a good place to start.

All of the teachings presented in this book are paths to living at peace within one's self and the world. How each of us handles the petty annoyances and major disputes in our individual lives adds to how the world will respond to this same issue.

In times like these, humanity's cruelty and ability to inflict suffering staggers the rational mind. Our behavior as a species is incomprehensible. In times like these, thank God for the teachings. When thousands of lives at once are lost to acts of violence, can there be anything more healing than the Buddhist path of compassion? The practice of Tonglen can be particularly helpful to you, and to soothe the suffering in the world. The Tibetan teachings on death and the bardo states of transition in between lives can help us understand our spiritual responsibility for holding sacred space for the dying and the dead. The Hindu teachings on the nature of the Kali Yuga we are immersed in can lend understanding of what we are up against. The Hindu understanding of worship to the "One God with many names" can be invaluable in helping to break down the biases and prejudices against the different names we all call God. Hinduism also helps us to understand Karma and the eternal nature of the soul. These teachings and all the meditation techniques offered by the Hindu path can be helpful in dark times. Returning to the teachings of the Tao can soothe our troubled souls and reveal a way to live in harmony with all of life. Tantra gives us the awareness and techniques for awakening, even in dark times.

The teachings are there for us in troubled times, like rafts that support us on turbulent waters. I am completing this writing during the outbreak of our worst-case fears and I know the teachings can be of assistance. It is my prayer that we learn to proactively engage the spiritual practices of the world, so they are not only rafts to rescue us in troubled times, but also become the fertile soil to grow our souls in times of peace and well-being.

INDEX